BETTY FEREGRINO

My Book Escape

Chapters of a Chicana

First edition

ISBN: 979-8-9997093-1-8

Editing by Lia Ottaviano
Cover art by Lucero Leon

This book was professionally typeset on Reedsy.
Find out more at reedsy.com

To my sister, who nurtured me.
To my husband, who encouraged me.

Contents

II   Part Two

Foreword

Before we begin, I need to acknowledge that some of the experiences shared in this memoir may be difficult to read. Out of respect for you, the reader, I want to offer this note so you can choose the pace and approach that feels right for you.

This book contains references to:

- Childhood sexual abuse
- Domestic violence
- Substance abuse and drug addiction
- Death and grief

These moments are part of my lived experience, and I've chosen to share them honestly. They do not define the entirety of my story, but they are threads of the tapestry that was my adolescent life.

If at any point you need to pause, put the book down, or step away, please honor that need.

While some pages reveal painful truths, I chose to release fear because this memoir is ultimately about resilience, healing, and hope.

Thank you for your support, and for allowing me to share my journey with you.

Prologue

This memory emerges in a small apartment, where the living room, hallway, and bathroom all lie shrouded in darkness. Magenta-colored, starry nebulous clouds encircle my periphery as I attempt to focus. And then, I hear it.

Shrieking and crying, a mix of fear and desperation, emanating from the same direction as a light. My curiosity piqued, my eyes followed the sound and the light to my right.

A dining room before me, centered with a 70s-style rattan chandelier, anchored with an oak table and chairs. A young girl, no older than seven, kneels backward on a chair facing the kitchen. Her tear-streaked face is blotchy, her eyes peeping under a curtain of thick dark bangs. Her hands clutch at the back of the chair, white knuckles, her terror palpable.

I follow her gaze, and I peer into the kitchen. A fair-colored woman, with long, dirty blonde hair falling in blunt bangs like the girl, stands pinned against the wall. She wears long white pajamas, her feet bare. Her attacker, a brown-skinned man wearing a white wife-beater, dark blue Dickies pants stained with paint splatter, and old, worn work boots, is beating her mercilessly.

The woman attempts to fight back and defend herself, pulling his hair with one fist, twisting to shred from his scalp, the other hand blocking and pushing him away. He overpowers her, pummeling her relentlessly.

The woman's belly is swollen, not from the blows, but from a near full-term pregnancy. The sight of it and the scene's brutality send bolts of fear shooting through me. And then, as if the violence could not escalate any further, the man rams his left knee into her abdomen. I want to look away, to flee, but it's as though I am paralyzed.

Suddenly, a dark shadowy figure of what appears to be the shape of a man materializes back in the living room. As I turn to get a better look at this figure, the moment ends.

The memory that haunts me is one that predates my own existence. I would often question if this was, in fact, a memory or a dream I conjured.

I corroborated this story by sharing it with my mom and sister. I couldn't understand why my mom was pregnant after me, yet I had no younger siblings. Mom and Erica both remembered that incident. I was the baby still forming in my mother's womb.

Introduction

I was in an apartment playing with other toddlers my age. We chased each other all around the living room. We shared and fought over toys while cartoons played on the TV in the background.

She took me to the bedroom and locked the door. She lay me on the bed, and I rested my head on the pillow. The made-up bed was pushed against the wall on one side, leaving only the opposite end for entry.

The sun's rays streamed into the bedroom through the window curtains and blinds, painting the room a hazy yellow. I could hear the other children still playing just on the other side of the bedroom door.

She removed her pants and underwear, her shirt still on. She made her way onto the bed and climbed over my tiny body. She was on her knees, one on each side of me. She stopped when her knees were on either side of my head.

She was covered in lots of dark pubic hair. Being underneath her blocked out the light, leaving me feeling like I was trapped in the dark.

She told me to hold out my tongue. As she maneuvered herself to settle over me in the position she wanted, her pubic hair roughly brushed against my face.

I didn't like what was happening, but when I tried to turn my face away, she'd tell me to stick my tongue out again. I didn't argue. I didn't know how to argue. I didn't understand.

I was choking on something stuck and irritating the back of my throat, but that didn't stop her. I attempted to push her off so that I could breathe, but I wasn't strong enough.

Finally, she stopped; it was over. She rolled off the bed and walked over to the bathroom. I could breathe again. I sat up on the bed, moved to let my legs hang off the side, and stared off into space. "What just happened?" I wondered.

She left the bathroom door open, and I could hear the sound of her urinating. I stood in the doorway, leaning on the frame. I reached my fingers into my mouth to try to remove the hair she left behind. I asked her what she had been doing. She didn't answer my question, but did say I wasn't allowed to tell anyone anything about what just happened.

I can't say who she was. A random woman who nannies the neighboring children? A family friend? A family member?

I was angry with my mother, for many years for this. I was left alone with this person; I wasn't protected.

At random moments throughout my life, this terrible memory would intrude on my peace and fill me with shame. I never spoke of it with anyone. I couldn't even bring myself to simply speak out loud about what happened when alone. I'd challenge myself to say it out loud when alone and in the dark, but I couldn't. At times, I tried to convince myself that it was just a nightmare. It never felt like I could reconcile that it wasn't my fault and I was, am, innocent. I was left in a permanent chokehold.

It is difficult to read about or watch rape scenes on film or TV because this memory is dredged up again. Writing this scene out, knowing numerous strangers would know my shame, was extremely distressing, as well as cathartic.

Distressing because it feels as though my body and soul are completely bare to the world. I imagine most readers won't relate; some may never see me the same.

Cathartic because I'm releasing the shame, and there are readers who *do* relate.

It wouldn't be until I was in my late thirties that I finally came to terms with what happened to me. I also was able to realize that this incident was not my mother's fault, and I was finally able to release what misdirected anger I had towards her for it.

I was sexually assaulted by a woman in my childhood. I was, am, a rape victim. But that's not all I am.

I'm a first-generation daughter, a sister, and a wife. I'm the first in my family to graduate from college, I'm a woman in leadership, and now I've added published indie author to my repertoire. I am part of the less than 8 percent of Latinos represented in the publishing industry.

I am a success!

I

PART 1

Before Death

Refugees

In late 1970s/early 1980s, my dad, Luis Antonio Aparicio, and one of his closest friends, Carlos, embarked on their journey to flee El Salvador with hopes for the chance at a better life in the United States. My dad and Carlos were so close that they came to call and introduce themselves as cousins. I grew up calling him mi Tío Carlos and his wife mi Tía Mirna. Their kids were my cousins and I never knew any different.

Pa and Tío Carlos, among many others, were desperate to escape the Civil War. Civilians were being massacred. Men, women and children. If you were out after 6pm, I was told, you would have been killed. If they'd stayed, that could have been their fate or, they would have been recruited into the army. It was do or die.
The United Nations (UN) estimates that the Salvadoran Civil War (1980–1992) killed more than 75,000 people, mostly non-combatants. The war also displaced over 1 million Salvadorans, about one-fifth of the population, many of whom fled to the United States.

Pa's family was also torn due to divorce. He and his siblings were separated during their youth. A few lived with their mother, a few lived with their father, and a few were adopted by extended family members. This caused emotional strains among parent and sibling relationships.

9

In a span of about eight days, Pa and Tío Carlos traveled from El Salvador across Guatemala and through Mexico. They stopped in Mexico City to visit two of my dad's sisters, who had migrated earlier, before making their way to Monterrey, Mexico and ultimately Houston, Texas, where they began to build new lives.

Through friends who had already migrated and settled in Houston, Pa made new friends and acquaintances. He found work at Bellaire Paint & Body. Named after the city of Bellaire, which sits in Southwest Houston. Owner of the business, Johnny Bang, immediately recognized my dad's potential. So much so that Johnny sponsored my dad to gain a Permanent Residential Immigration Status and to attend English language classes. In 1984, when Johnny decided to sell the Bellaire shop and open in far north Tomball, he asked my dad to join him, and my dad followed.

While working for Johnny, my dad met Jesus Santana; everyone called him "Jesse," but my dad nicknamed him "Duke." One day, Pa received a call from his sisters, whom he briefly visited in Mexico. Sonia and Estella had prematurely crossed the border, and they owed the "coyote" (migrant smuggler) money for passage. Pa was livid. He yelled through the receiver, reminding them he had directed them to wait and not to cross since he hadn't saved up enough money. Sonia responded that it was too late and that he needed to send the funds immediately. Sonia passed the phone to the coyote. My dad asked for a few hours and instructions on how to send the money. Immediately after getting off the phone, he contacted Jesse, aka "Duke," and begged for a loan. He feared for his sisters' safety and was desperate. Together, Pa and Duke scraped up enough money for the coyote, and his sisters made it to Houston safely. At that point, my dad was responsible for keeping his sisters. He took them to the apartment he shared with a few other male roommates.

Not too long after, he discovered Jesse and Sonia had begun dating, and Pa became enraged. He threatened Jesse and accused him of taking his sister as a form of payment since he hadn't yet been able to repay the loan.

My mother, Francisca S. Feregrino, was born on a small ranch in the state of Michoacán, Mexico. My abuela was a stay-at-home wife to my abuelo, who made firewood and was somewhat of the local spiritual leader. Because my abuelos' home was in a small settlement in the mountain region and not much had been developed in that area, there was no formal school system. Therefore, my mother and most of her family were not formally educated.

While my mother was a young girl, my grandmother sent her to live with extended family. Sadly, this left my mother vulnerable. She was abused by her male uncles and cousins. When she brought this information to her mom, her mother blamed her, a mere child, for the abuse. My mother threatened to inform her dad, and my grandmother slapped her in retaliation.

Mom was closer to her father than she was to her mother, and she felt that her mother was jealous of them for it. Eventually, due to the threat and abuse, Mom was relocated to live with other family in Mexico City. Sadly, she was no safer there.

One day, an older guy approached her and her cousin, inviting them to hang out another night. They accepted. On the night she and her cousin were to meet up with him, her cousin was a no-show, leaving her alone. Mom felt she may have been set up. The man took advantage of her.

My mother was forced to demand that her boyfriend make an honest woman out of her because young girls had little-to-no rights or options back then, and so they married. Unfortunately, he turned out to be an alcoholic who would not provide for her and their new baby. She made the difficult decision to leave her baby, Erica, in the care of her sister so that she could find work beyond the border. Because of this, Erica never had a relationship with her biological father.

Mom migrated to the U.S. alone as a young adult without knowing anyone or even the English language. Her first job was as a live-in nanny, and when she raised enough money, she sent for Erica to join her.

In the U.S., Mom left behind her birth-given name and adopted a new name, "Angela."

Mom loved the children she cared for, and through their care, was able to slowly pick up the English language. She quickly fell in love with the American Rock music scene, listening to artists like Queen, Prince, and David Bowie, and was excited to be a part of a whole new world.

In early 1984, Mom and Erica moved into a new apartment complex. La Terraza apartments, located in the Braeswood neighborhood of Southwest Houston, housed many immigrant families. Immigrants from places such as Mexico, Central America, and Vietnam. It was here that Mom met a neighbor, Gloria Aparicio. Gloria later introduced her brother, Luis, to her new friend Angela.

Saint Francis, The Devil & An Angel

When Mom went into labor with me, she and Pa took the Metro bus to Jefferson Davis Hospital. During my cesarean delivery, Mom coded. She had a near-death and out-of-body experience. She would recount my birthday, remembering having a top view looking down on her body while doctors and nurses scrambled to revive her.

During this moment, she prayed. She asked God and the Virgin Mary to save her so that she could take care of her children. She feared my father, a drug addict, would sell me if she didn't return. She made a promise to the Virgin Mary that she would take care of all the animals in return for saving her life. After her prayer, she woke up back in her body and had a new baby girl. Pa had already decided my name - Betty Stephanie.

"Why don't I have the last name Aparicio?" I asked.

One look at me, a puffy-faced newborn baby, and my dad accused my mother of having an affair with another man, so he refused to sign my birth certificate.
My father was charismatic, good-humored, and when able, generous. But, my father was also a thief, a drug addict, and a domestic abuser. As much as I loved him, there is no erasing the fact that at times, he was monstrous.

13

When they still lived together, there were moments when my dad was so raving mad and physically abusive towards my mom that it forced Mom to take us girls and flee for safety. Mom once shared,

"Your dad was so crazy, he would pour sand in front of the door so that he could check to see if a man left footprints! And he would threaten to kill me if he found any."

Since Mom had no family nearby, she had no choice but to seek refuge at a local Women's Shelter. We didn't grow up like your typical Hispanic family, having a small community of aunts, uncles, and cousins. For the most part, it was just the three of us.

Once, during my toddler years, Mom, Erica, and I were forced to run. Fleeing the apartment complex my aunts and their families lived in, we made a mad dash to the car. I quickly scrambled into the backseat, cowering behind my mom, who then dove into the driver's seat, swiftly slamming the door shut. Mom slightly rolled down the window to yell back at my dad, who was chasing behind us. In a state of absolute fury, he began punching the window, shouting and cursing. We thought the window would shatter at any moment.

My petite aunts, Tía Estella and Tía Sonia, both attempted to pull his arms back in hopes it would prevent his fists from making contact, screaming over him, begging him to stop, and pushing him away from the car. But his strength was no match.

I screeched and cried in terror, sparking the nerves in my muscles to begin convulsions, wishing it would end.

Pa pushed his arm through and attempted to grab Mom through the window gap, forcing her to lean away, far into Erica's passenger seat, and struggling to reverse out of the parking lot. In what felt like a miracle and an eternity later, Mom was finally able to shift gears and sped away.

My pants were wet. I worried Mom would get mad at me for peeing in the car. I didn't pee myself on purpose, so I didn't mention my accident. That menacing scene was enough to deal with. We rode back to our apartment in silence.

In another instance, still a young toddler, Pa drove the two of us to the Burger King in Bellaire, where Mom worked. I was seated in the front passenger seat, and I watched Mom walk out of the side employee entrance near the drive-thru to meet us. After a short conversation, they began to argue. Mom, visibly frustrated, turned and walked away, back towards the door she exited out of. Suddenly, Pa slammed his foot down and floored the gas pedal. The engine revved loudly in reaction, and the car charged forward in her direction with the tires screeching against the pavement. Mom, hearing the car accelerate, looked back over her shoulder to see us barreling toward her in an attempt to run her down. I watched her eyes grow wide in shock and fear, matching my own. I clutched onto the seat cushion underneath me, hoping he would stop. She spun back around and sprinted to the door. Pa slammed on the brakes, and the door slammed shut behind her. She narrowly made it inside.

When the TV show COPS was on, I was always a little anxious. They filmed a portion of this docu-series in Houston, so recognizing this was in our city, I was apprehensive suspecting I would catch my dad in an episode.

While there is photographic evidence that my parents lived together when I was a baby, I have no memory of them raising me as a couple. I only remember being raised by a single mom and an older sister. But mainly by my older sister.

One weekend, Mom took a trip to Galveston with her friends, leaving Erica and me home alone. Erica was left in charge of my care, even though she was just a 10-year-old child herself. Come Monday morning, Mom hadn't yet returned. Feeling she had no choice, Erica brought me to school with her.

I accompanied Erica to her fifth-grade class, where I sat in a student's desk right beside my sister, our desks pressed together. Erica's teacher gave me crayons to color with and kept me occupied for the day.

Throughout the day, I dropped the crayons on the floor, and the nice Black boy seated nearby would help pick them up for me. I was excited to be around my sister and the other big kids in school. I was enamored with the classroom setup and decor and the size of the school campus. I looked forward to being in school on my own someday to experience class like Erica did on a daily basis.

It was a miracle the teacher didn't call Child Protective Services.

That winter, Houston received a miracle: we had a snow day. Or, at least I assumed it was snow. Excited to see snow for the first time, I ran out of the apartment looking for the piles and blankets of white stuff. Not realizing sleet turned to ice on the front porch, I unintentionally slid across a few feet before losing my balance and slamming down on my backside. Erica immediately appeared by my side to console me. She picked me up, pulled my sweatpants down a bit, and rubbed my blushed bottom while I cried in agony. She pulled my pants back up, hugged me tight, verbally consoled me, and rubbed my back until my cries turned into soft sobs. My tears stopped, and my breathing calmed, with only a few hitches here and there. It was my sister's, not our mother's, maternal instinct that always comforted me.

The next year, I was enrolled in preschool, and every weekday morning, Erica would wake me from my slumber to help me prepare for the

16

day. She would brush my long, thick hair up into a ponytail and take the elastic hair ties with colorful plastic balls on the ends to secure my hair for the day. During the process, the force of pulling my hair back would hurt, and I would want to cry, but it would soon be over.

Erica would turn the television on as background entertainment, keeping the volume down low, while I ate whatever she prepared for me. Sometimes it was cereal, sometimes it was scrambled eggs with chopped hot dogs or bologna. Typically, episodes of *Saved by the Bell* reruns were on. I can still hear and sing the theme song in my head. If that show wasn't on, Looney Tunes cartoons were.

We sat quietly in front of the glowing television, which cast light into the living room when the sun was not yet up, careful not to wake Mom. Still grumpy and half asleep, Erica sat at my feet to gently slip on my socks, followed by each shoe. Would I bother lifting my leg to support the weight and help her out? No, and she never complained or chastised me. She enjoyed caring for me, as if I were her own.

Virgo Moon

The Virgin Maiden represents Virgo in the zodiac constellation. For those born under a Virgo Moon, astrologers predict that the relationship between mother and child will be strained. Either the mother will be too critical of the child, such as demanding better grades in school, or the mother won't fully nurture the child. Coincidentally, my sister and I were both born under Virgo Moons. Her relationship with Mom reflects the former and mine the latter.

My sister had more of a capricious relationship with our mom. Because Erica was the oldest child, she took the brunt of Mom's frustrations and, therefore, shielded me, leaving me to often be ignored.

One morning, Erica missed her school bus. Too afraid to wake Mom to figure out a ride to school, she decided to avoid her wrath and simply walk. Mom always slept in and hated being awakened early. If we woke her, she would rise in a foul mood, griping and accusing us of not letting her rest, resulting in her experiencing headaches and pain.

Erica's walking commute to school was forty-five minutes long, and the route she needed to take forced her to cross the busy Westpark Tollway during rush hour.

Erica was responsible for my care as well as keeping the house clean. While I can't recall all the many altercations between Erica and Mom during my toddler years, I can recall some pleasant moments I had with my mom.

On the rare moments when it was just Mom and me, we would lie in bed watching television. We had a love for the PBS channel. We enjoyed catching Bollywood music videos featuring beautiful, ornate costumes, large, choreographed dance numbers, and vibrant colors. All of these elements combined were more than enough to forget the fact that we had no clue what they were singing about, as the music was in another language. The acting helped provide context, and they were mostly love stories, it seemed.

We laughed watching Mr. Bean and his crazy adventures. His antics vaguely reminded me of a male version of the Amelia Bedelia books. Mr. Bean's character never spoke a word; instead, he only mumbled and used body language to communicate. We laughed at how Mr. Bean was oblivious to the trail of disruption he naively created.

Another British show we really enjoyed was *Keeping Up Appearances*. In this British sitcom, the protagonist, Hyacinth Bucket which she pronounced Bouquet to elevate the name lived to impress. In nearly every episode, Hyacinth tries her best to prove how upperclass she is while driving her obliging husband and everyone else mad. Mom and I would laugh at the absurd and ridiculous situations these characters landed in. The fact that the female lead tried so hard to fit in was something we both felt was silly and unnecessary.

When Mom gave herself manicures featuring fire-engine red polish on long, almond-shaped nails, I would take her hand and carefully run the tip of my tongue across the smooth lacquer painted nails. I'd then run them back across my lips to avoid leaving any trace of saliva. Having the opportunity to be that close to her was comforting, as it wasn't very often.

Mom enjoyed going to Burger King for lunch, then taking the Metro public transit bus to Hermann Park, located in the Museum District. During a particular visit, while Mom, Erica, and I were walking near the ponds, a single duck caught Mom's attention. It seemed injured. After a couple of attempts, Mom and Erica were able to capture the duck and inspect it. Sadly, they discovered its wing to be disabled, confirming their suspicions. Next thing you know, we were riding the Metro bus back to our neighborhood, duck in tow. She was sure to keep her promise to the Virgin Mary and take care of the animals.

In our apartment, we had a fish tank filled with small fish and two of those sucker fish that help filter water and keep the glass clean. We also had two cats, Mom's orange tabby and Erica's grey tuxedo cat, Kida.

Mom fashioned a homemade splint for the duck's wing. Using a metal hanger and leftover cloth found in her sewing kit, she gently wrapped the duck's injured wing with hopes it would heal back to its proper shape. Although my mother wasn't formally educated, Mom was quite ingenious when it came to helping care for animals.

Erica filled the bathtub with water for the duck's temporary home, while Mom used the green handheld mesh-net to scoop fish from the tank and transport them to the tub. The duck took to it, well, like a duck to water.

Eventually, the duck ate all our fish. Mom began making recurring trips to the pet shop to purchase more live fish to feed the duck.

Anytime we needed to shower, we'd have to remove the duck from the tub and set it on the restroom floor, drain, and scrub the tub with Comet before getting in ourselves. Then, another good rinse before we could refill the tub for the duck again.

Mom's cat would occasionally sneak into the restroom if someone didn't shut the doors properly. It may have often been me, as children aren't as aware of being careful with their surroundings. The shocked and frightened duck would flap its wings, causing more damage and delaying its healing. There were times Mom's cat would sneak into the bedroom if someone forgot to close the doors, and would attack Erica's cat, Kida. Once, it happened in my top bunk bed while Kida slept with me. The cats began to wrestle, hissing and growling, biting and scratching, and fumbling like the cartoon quick-speed tumbleweeds until they both dropped and fell to the ground. Mom favored her cat over Erica's, ultimately getting rid of Kida altogether. This broke my sister's heart.

Finally, the duck healed up, so we returned to Hermann Park, dropped it off where it was found, and said our goodbyes.

Doña Marie

Serendipitously, Mom met a new neighbor named Doña Marie. They became fast friends. Doña Marie wasn't happy with her living situation, and so Mom invited her to move in with us instead. In lieu of paying rent, they bartered services. Doña Marie became our nanny in the evenings so Mom could work nights, and, because she was an older woman, she sort of became a maternal figure to my mom.

On occasion, Doña Marie brought fresh Mexican sweet bread, and Mom would prepare Folgers coffee with warmed milk to serve them. For my drink, she added Chocolate Nesquick powder to the mug and stirred in hot milk with a small pour of coffee. I would then take a Chocolate Concha to dip into the mocha and take a sopping bite, followed by a sip of my drink. It made me feel special that she thought of serving me a personalized mug.

Doña Marie never learned to speak English, and I only spoke English, so whenever she would attempt to converse with me, I would look to Erica or Mom and ask, "What did she say?"

After this occurred repeatedly, Doña Marie grew frustrated.

"Wha' she'say, wha' she'say, siempre con wha' she'say!" she would snap.

Then she'd complain to my mom about my inability to speak Spanish and yell at me to say that I needed to learn Spanish. These interactions would annoy me, and I began to enjoy not being able to fully converse with her.

While Mom was away at work, Erica and I still had energy to burn, and not yet wanting to sleep, we entertained ourselves. We would play with our Barbies and spend what felt like hours setting up the Barbie house. We prepped each room of the house: kitchen, living room, bedroom, etc. We were crafty and used whatever objects we could find, such as shoe boxes, white plastic pizza savers from the center of the to-go boxes as tables or chairs, and other random trinkets to make the dream home. By the time we completed our setup, we were too spent to actually play with the dolls, and would pack everything up to put it all away. We would then turn on the TV in the living room, mock the actors we were watching, throw snacks at the screen, and laugh.

Sometimes, we would take a boombox stereo, insert a blank cassette tape, and attempt to record our farts. We thought this was hilarious! We would try so hard to force out the gas that we would have to run to the restroom to avoid peeing ourselves. When we got too loud, Doña Marie would barge into the room and yell, "Cálmate ya! Quédate dormidos ahora!" Which would only cause us to laugh some more.

One night, I heard someone in the shower. Assuming it was Erica, I quietly snuck into the restroom and took a peek behind the curtain to try and scare her. But I was the one who got scared. I was greeted by a FULL MOON! Doña Marie was in all her glory, facing the shower head and rinsing her hair, utterly unaware that I was staring right at her backside. Her bottom displayed a broad, textured landscape of dimples and craters, reminiscent of our moon's surface. At first, I was shocked because I was not expecting to see her butt, and she wasn't a blood relative, but after I processed what I was looking at, I caught the giggles. I swiftly swung the shower curtain shut and ran out of the restroom, holding my hand to my mouth to keep the laughter tightly trapped inside. When I made it out to the bedroom, I laughed out loud, holding my tummy and slapping the bed mattress.

Later that night, I shared with Mom and Erica what I had seen. Mom laughed a little but told me I shouldn't spy on people in the shower or make fun of Doña Marie. Erica just laughed with me.

Doña Marie was a small, petite woman, and as I grew taller, she seemed to get smaller. She had terribly aged skin. The kind that was dry, lacking collagen, deeply wrinkled, and riddled with age spots. She had long wispy, gray hair always set in a tight bun and wore matronly outfits. She always looked extremely old to me, so I dubbed her "the ancient one." Whenever we got to hang out with my dad and her name came up, Pa would ask in surprise, "She's still alive?!"

Doña Marie often traveled back to Mexico to visit family and friends. She would receive invitations from many requesting her presence at their daughter's Quinceañeras or weddings, and journey back to celebrate the holidays. Because of her frequent trips, whenever Mom grew frustrated with me leaving my toys around and not putting them away, she would pack them up and give them to Doña Marie, who would take them across the border to other children. Same with the clothes we outgrew. It would upset me that these unknown escuincles had my toys.

Doña Marie didn't own a car, so she relied on the Metro bus service to get around town. And around town, she went. From time to time, she would have a fall. So often, we would hear women from the neighborhood report the incidents to my mom. She would even fall on sidewalks. It was very worrisome. My mom eventually contacted Doña

Marie's son to warn and encourage him to make time to chauffeur his mom around.

Come Christmas season, I was in my mother's bedroom when I saw a large, oversized object covered with a bed sheet. Being as small as I was, the object looked like a small mountain with varied levels of topography.

I was curious to know what could be hiding under the sheet. When I got close enough, I lifted the sheet for a peek and all I found was a large, black plastic wheel. Not a second later, the sheet was quickly yanked out of my hand and pulled back down. I was scolded by Doña Marie for peeking so I stormed off. I didn't like her telling me what to do.

On Christmas Day, I was gifted a Power Wheels Jeep Wrangler. That's what was hidden under the sheet. It was used, but I was none the wiser, and it was one of the most incredible things I can remember ever receiving. While most girls wanted pink bikes with glitter tassels, roller skates, or Power Wheels with rainbow stickers, I wasn't that kind of girly girl. Like my mom, who drove a badass Camaro, I preferred something cooler. My Jeep was fire-engine red with a flaming bald eagle decal on the hood. The hood featured latches that you could open to reveal the inner workings. The dusty rechargeable battery lived here, and I would have to remove it daily to plug it in for a recharge. It felt as significant as when my dad would work on real cars, tinkering under the hood. I did the same thing to care for my vehicle, so I felt as cool as my mom and dad.

Other kids in the complex had Power Wheels too, and we loved racing one another. There was one girl my age, a very pretty Black girl with long, thin braids. I considered her to be rich because her clothes and shoes were always so pressed and clean, and she always had fun toys or accessories. Not to mention, her Power Wheel was a fancy

Corvette! It may have even been a Barbie version because it was very pink.

Her Corvette was sweet. When she popped her hood, her "engine" had cables and connectors in fancy, bright colors along with a large, clean, shiny battery. That clean and shiny battery must've been a supercharger because her Corvette had power!

We would line up our cars to race, and at the count, she would take off like a speeding bullet. I floored the pedal as hard as I could, but I could never win. Sometimes, most times, my battery would die on me. Although I was embarrassed at how my car failed, it never changed my love for my Jeep.

While driving my Jeep inside the apartment, I began to hear Doña Marie scolding me. To show her I was upset, and in hopes to shut her up, I threw the gear into reverse, slammed the pedal for full speed, ramming the back of my Jeep right into her. The Jeep hit Doña Marie's legs, and I quickly shifted back into Drive, peeling forward, laughing maniacally. I drove straight into my mom's bedroom to lock the door.

I was only five years old, and I had maliciously attempted some form of attempted vehicular manslaughter. I wonder where or whom I could have learned that from?

I'm sure I caused little to no damage, but in that moment, I wanted to cause *all* the damage.

Doña Marie had a habit of making me feel less than. For one, she was always griping about my inability to speak Spanish. Excuse me, but if no one took the time to actually teach me, what choice did I have? I hated watching Spanish television channels. The novelas had terrible acting and predictable story lines. The news was gory and depressing to watch. The movies dubbed in Spanish irked my nerves for an unknown reason. Even Plaza Sesamo annoyed me.

My thought process as a child was, if Mom, Pa, and Erica all spoke to me in English, as well as all my teachers at school, what was the point of learning?

Then, there were the nicknames she gave me: Prieta, Morena, and Negra. My skin tone was darker than Mom's and Erica's; her referring to me by these names constantly felt like she was insinuating that my skin was *too* dark. Some may suggest those nicknames were just terms of endearment, but while growing up in the 90s, being brown-skinned wasn't very popular. There was little to no representation of brown skin on TV, in movies, or in magazines.

The kids at school sometimes asked if I was adopted because my mom, sister, and I didn't look alike. I felt like the ugly duckling.

Finally, there was the gossiping about my dad. Doña Marie and Mom would have conversations when I would hear, "y el papá"." Based on their tone and body language, I knew it was about my dad, and it wasn't anything good. I didn't appreciate them speaking ill of my father. Once, my mom noticed me eavesdropping on their conversation, and she stopped to say in English, "She'll grow up to resent him."

Stepdad

My parents never legally married, but in 1990, my mom did marry someone: Javier Orneales. Javier was a tall, light-skinned Chicano with dark hair, dark-colored eyes, and dark-rimmed glasses similar to Superman's Clark Kent. Not at all my mom's type. It's a wonder what attracted her to him in the first place.

Mom met Javier at the cantina where she was working. When Mom brought Javier home to meet us, Erica wanted nothing to do with another one of Mom's boyfriends, so she ignored him. Suddenly, in retaliation, Mom slapped Erica right across the face for her impertinence.

Javier served in one of the military branches. On his right forearm, he displayed this military pride as a large tattoo. This tattoo depicted a soldier dressed in total army fatigue featuring green and brown camouflage, complete with a helmet, a rifle strapped over the shoulder, and fitted combat boots.

When I first met Javier, he asked, "Do you want to see a trick? I can make him march," referring to the aforementioned tattoo soldier.

Intrigued, I asked him, "How?"

Javier proceeded to hold out his forearm, clench his fist, and move his fingers, manipulating the muscles in his forearm to move in a manner that gave the appearance of the soldier marching. I smiled and laughed in delight. I liked Javier.

Supposedly, they hooked up the first night they met. Javier over-shared that information with Erica after he and my mom found themselves in a couple's fight one drunken night. What caused the argument, I don't know, but I'm sure alcohol only exacerbated their issue.

Mom locked herself in the bathroom while Javier lingered outside the door, begging and crying. At one point, he knelt down on the ground, removing his wallet from his back pocket and rummaging through it to remove a photo. It was a photo of the two of them. He slid the picture under the door, pleading with Mom to pick it up and look at it.

My mom was a beauty. In our community, people referred to her as "Güera" or "La Americana," and other Spanish descriptors that likened her to being a white American woman. She had long, wavy, bleached blonde hair. Her face featured a high cheekbone structure, and she carried herself with long, Barbie-like legs that she would consistently show off in miniskirts or dresses fitted with heels. She also had a perky butt. She was just about every guy's dream girl. It was the early 90s and her look was a very Pamela Anderson vibe. All this to say, her beauty drove every guy she dated to feel insecure and dread that they could never keep the gorgeous bird caged.

The novelty of this novela-esque episode wore off, and now it was boring to watch. It was late, so Erica and I went to bed.

Javier was a chef at Brennan's restaurant located in central Houston. This Creole and Southern hospitality-driven establishment was a fancy place I thought only rich people dined at.

After their "I Do's" at a local Harris County courthouse, Mom and Javier hosted their wedding reception at Brennan's courtyard. Mom wore a short-length, above-the-knee, beaded, lacey white dress with matching gloves and a short veil. Very Madonna. I don't remember who from his side of the family was in attendance, but it had to have been a small turnout. Erica only recalls meeting Javier's brother. We, of course, had no extended family in attendance.

Late evenings, mostly on weekends, I would stay up past my bedtime to hang out while Javier watched *The Benny Hill Show*. I'd be playing with my toys when I'd look up at the TV and see an old man chasing a woman with a skirt tucked into the backside of her underwear. I didn't get the point of the skit or any of the humor really, but the actresses had beautiful figures, like my mom's, so I guessed that's why people watched it.

For Mom's birthday, Javier decided to bake her a cake. Javier drove Erica and me to pick up the supplies from our local Kroger grocery store. The supplies included a non-traditional aluminum baking pan, vanilla Betty Crocker cake mix, orange colored icing, candles, and other baking specialties. The cake batter took the shape of Garfield, the heavy weight orange male tabby who was a famous Sunday newspaper comic strip turned TV cartoon. I don't feel Mom particularly cared for the Garfield cartoon, but we did have her Orange Tabby.

For Mom's cake, Javier used a specific icing tip to create individual, textured icing dollops in rows that, when using your imagination, resembled fur. I sat, elbows and upper torso on the table, and watched him repeat the painstaking process of squeezing out each drop of icing to match all the hundreds of other drops. Unfortunately, I was a squirmy girl, and so, to stop me from shaking the dining table and ruining his process, he assigned Erica to relocate me to the living room and distract me with some child-friendly activity. It was an endearing labor of love. Unfortunately, I don't remember Mom's reaction to gauge if she appreciated the custom Garfield cake or not.

That school year, at Sneed Elementary, the kindergarten class was putting on a recital. The kids and I in music class practiced the same song repeatedly for days, maybe even weeks. After so many plays, I began to memorize and sing along with the song's intro, which was about dinosaurs. I knew the words so well that the teachers identified me along with two other kids who memorized the lyrics, and the faculty decided it would be a fun treat to have the three of us open the show. We learned that the three of us would be wearing dinosaur costumes! I could barely contain my excitement the whole way home. After my stop, I jumped off the bus and ran to my apartment. Seeing Javier first, I rushed inside to jump onto his lap and tell him my big news. I was going to be a star! He was excited and congratulated me.

On recital day, my two classmates and I put on our costumes fitted with toy guitars. When the curtains opened, I scanned the audience and spotted Javier and my mom sitting in the left rear rows in front of our stage. Instantly, I swelled with pride and joy. I always assumed Javier encouraged and probably pressured my mom to attend. I felt this way because it took place during the school day, and my mom usually slept through the day, and also because she never attended another daytime recital or school activity again. She was not the typical PTA/PTO program mom.

Javier took us to visit Galveston. At the beach, Erica and I ventured into the ocean for a swim. As we waded deeper into the ocean, we were taken over by an unexpected and strong wave. I went under and swallowed the brown, briny water. It immediately came back up. I vomited straight into the ocean suds a mix with my semi-digested lunch. The vomit came up and out of my nose, singeing along the way.

To ensure we didn't waste the trip, or remain traumatized, and build my confidence in the ocean, Erica carried me back into the ocean. For moral support, I brought my Barbie with me.

Resting on her hip, one arm wrapped around her shoulders, we waded back in. I could feel her wet, sticky hair on the skin of my arm. The stickiness was undoubtedly from the mixture of sand and saltwater. Wading around, I dip Barbie in for a dive and bring her back up for air.

And then there was pain! Stinging, burning pain! Throwing my arms in the air and flinging Barbie in the process, I screeched at the top of my lungs and began jerking uncontrollably. Hysterically crying, I wanted out of the water. Erica struggled to keep me from slipping from her grasp and losing me in the waves.

Jellyfish. It wrapped its tentacles around my wrist and thigh, also grabbing and stinging Erica in the process. Erica quickly staggered through the waves to get us back on shore to be examined. Charred burn marks were left on my skin, while Erica had red welts. Erica was so worried about me that she couldn't focus on herself. She didn't scream or cry.

Once I calmed down from the pain, I realized Barbie was missing. "My Barbie!" I shrieked. That day, Barbie became a free mermaid.

Shortly after, we packed up to return home. When we pulled up to the apartment complex and parked, Erica and I headed to the pool. Our neighbor friends were there having a good time, as evidenced by their laughs and boisterous voices. I felt comfortable swimming in a clear pool with no sea monsters, but the chlorine stung my burns.

Broken Family

When Mom first met Javier, we lived in a one-bedroom apartment. In the center of the bedroom was the large bed for my mom. Near the foot of her bed was a small twin-sized bed for our nanny, Doña Marie, and to the right was our bunk bed. Erica had the bottom bunk, and I had the top. When Javier moved in, Doña Marie moved out, and Erica would occasionally sleep in the single twin bed.

I once woke up early when I heard a consistent squeaking noise coming from inside the room, so I rolled over to look down. Javier lay on his back, legs, and arms outstretched like a starfish in the center of the bed, glasses off. He wore a white T-shirt and white underwear, or what I call "manties," which stands for male panties. It was probably this sight that forever convinced me to believe men should only be allowed to wear boxers or boxer briefs. No exceptions! My dad wore boxers, and real men wore boxers. My mom was wearing a nightie and was sitting on top of him, rocking back and forth. I felt embarrassed and confused, not fully understanding what I had witnessed. I quietly rolled back over, pretending to be asleep.

Thankfully, we soon moved into a two-bedroom, second-level apartment in the Gulfton area of Southwest Houston. Erica and I shared a room, while Mom and Javier had the other. Erica and I did a terrible job of keeping our room clean, and often you couldn't see the floor under the sea of clothes, toys, shoes, and junk piled from corner to corner. But we liked it this way.

The community at Lantern Village had a small convenience store located on the grounds, and next door to that was a dry cleaning shop. Occasionally, my sister and I would grab my mom's "penny-thing," a vase she used to collect spare change, and count out how much we needed to buy snacks. My favorite snack to buy was a creamy fudge chocolate ice cream popsicle.

On our first visit, we tried to pay the clerk in coins, which consisted of hundreds of pennies, along with several nickels and dimes, and possibly a few quarters. The clerk, annoyed, handed us brown wrapper rolls. Before leaving with the merchandise, we had to collect and fit our change into these labeled paper rolls. Once we appropriately filled the rolls so the coins would be as good as cash, we counted enough to cover the cost of our coveted snacks. Afterward, we devised a plan to speed up the purchasing process.

Erica stayed inside the apartment to roll more coins, while I commuted to and from the convenience store with snacks. To save me the time and effort of climbing up and down the stairs, Erica created the ingenious system of fitting a small red bucket with a long piece of string and lowering the bucket from our bedroom window to the ground level where I waited to exchange goods. I would take the newly rolled coins out and place the snacks in; she'd then hoist the bucket back up, and off I went to return to the store with a new snack list. Good thing the community convenience store was in our same parking lot instead of on the other side of the street—and no stranger danger incidents to report of either.

Living here, we tried to fall into an ordinary routine. With Javier, we would play games together as a family. My favorite at the time was the

Candy Land board game. But this slow life wasn't making my mom happy.

Mom was still working at the cantina, Erica was amid her rebellious teenage years, and Javier wasn't earning much as a chef. One night at about 2 am, Javier woke my sister and me to join him in the car to pick up my mom from the cantina after work.

When we returned to the apartment and Javier parked the car, I got out of the driver's side behind Javier, while Erica was slowly exiting the passenger side. My mom, drunk and frustrated that Erica was moving too slowly (because she was half asleep), slapped my sister to wake her up and rush her. Erica, shocked and slightly delirious, reacted by slapping Mom back. This wasn't intentional; it was an automatic reaction, and Erica immediately regretted it.

Mom became enraged. She began assaulting Erica verbally, lunging at her, and even threatening to kill her. Mom's behavior triggered me because she was in the same lunatic state my dad would be in during his fits of rage.

My mom continued yelling and chased Erica around the car, even while wearing six-inch heels. Erica tried to evade my mom and get back to the apartment safely, but Mom continued to chase and block her. Javier attempted to grab and hold my mom back, but he couldn't contain her. Mom wouldn't relent. By then, it was nearly 3am, and we were disturbing the peace and sleep of neighboring renters. Javier had no choice but to call the police. I stood there crying, fearing my mom would succeed at catching and killing my sister.

Then the police came knocking on our door. The two officers found Erica and brought her back home. In stern, authoritative voices, the officers told my mother she wasn't allowed to abuse Erica physically, and she had to let her into the home. They also warned her that if she didn't comply with their orders, they would arrest her.

The presence of the police, along with their tone towards Mom, frightened me, and I began to cry again. I didn't want my mom to go to jail. Javier held me on his lap to comfort me.

Erica, finally able, walked inside, circumventing my mom, grabbed me by my hand, and led me to our room. She shut the door behind us and immediately locked the door.

Sadly, Javier and Mom weren't married long. After their separation, we believe it was Javier who filed a report with Harris County Child Protective Services.

I was in my first-grade class when my teacher informed me that I had been summoned to the principal's office. A principal's aide led me to a conference room with two adults I didn't recognize, seated inside. The aide then turned to leave and shut the door behind her. The two strangers gestured for me to sit across from them, formally introduced themselves, and informed me that they needed to ask me questions about my family.

Where did my mom work? How often did I see my dad? Was I being taken care of? Did I ever witness my dad use drugs? Did my dad ever hurt me? It was all very intrusive. I felt vulnerable, anxious, and fearful because I thought I was in trouble or I would say something that would get me in trouble. Or worse, put my family in jeopardy.

I would often hear stories about my dad being in jail, and I assumed his being locked away in the county jail was what kept him away so often; I didn't want that to happen to anyone else in my family. When I got home from school that day, I recounted what had happened to Mom and Erica. They spoke quietly between themselves and assured me not to worry about it. I never heard from those interrogating adults again.

The last time I saw Javier was when the school nurse called him. He was still listed as an emergency contact on my school records. The nurse informed him that they couldn't get a hold of my mom and that I needed to be picked up early and taken home because I had thrown up in class. Javier arrived in the familiar white Geo Storm coupe and drove me home. When Mom answered the door, she looked at him, looked at me, and rolled her eyes, visibly annoyed, before storming away. My heart sank. She was mad at me. I walked in first, head down, and Javier followed. I set my backpack down and walked to the sofa, reaching for the remote control to turn on the TV in hopes of finding cartoons. Mom was obviously going to be ignoring me now and would not be offering me any comfort. I didn't know how long it would be before Erica got home, but I knew she would take care of me once she did.

Javier followed my mom to the bedroom. She argued and snapped at him enough times to deplete any tiny shred of hope he had of reconciling.

He said goodbye, walked out the door, and I never saw him again. I was too young to understand that at that moment, it really was goodbye forever. Mom never explained why their relationship ended. None of her other boyfriends treated me the way Javier did. Javier genuinely cared for me. I often wished he would come back into our lives. It was a nice feeling, having a whole family instead of a broken one. I sincerely hope he lived a happy life after us.

Ringling Bros and Barnum & Bailey

My dad did what most kids wish their parents would do: he brought me to the circus. The Ringling Brothers and Barnum & Bailey Circus returned to Houston with their new main attraction: the birth and addition of two baby elephants, Romeo and Juliette. This show had been advertised everywhere! You'd see it on television, on billboards, and in grocery stores. You'd hear about it on the radio and even from other kids at school. I had never been to the circus before, so I was thrilled when Pa told me he was taking me.

The circus took place at what was then known as The Summit. This arena held major national concerts and was home to the Houston Rockets basketball team.

That night, we rode to the circus with my cousins and uncle. We kids bounced all over the backseat, filled with eager jitters and giggles. After parking in the garage, we walked over to the venue. Once inside, we had to split up to find seats in separate sections. "We'll meet them after the show ends," Pa said.

My senses were overwhelmed as Pa and I walked through the stadium halls. There were thousands of people and other kids. Countless concession stands lined the outer arena, one after the other, filled with food offerings and filling the air with the aroma of buttery popcorn, juicy hot dogs, crunchy fried chicken, flavored ice cream with warm cones, and more!

Nestled between the food and beverage options were colorful, eye-catching merch stands. The stands drew in children like flies to a bug zapper. Poor parents didn't know what they were up against. They sold plushies, light-up toys, spinning toys, helium-filled balloons, and noisemakers. The branded products included tees, backpacks, pens and pencils, mugs, notepads, erasers, coloring books, and more. But one item in particular, caught my eye: a pink light-up toy that you held in your hand like a scepter. With the push of a button, the plastic sphere on top would spin fast, releasing multi-colored lights with dazzling effects. It reminded me of Sailor Moon's scepter, and I was enamored with it. And to my surprise, Pa noticed and walked us over to the register to purchase the memento for me. I felt like the richest kid alive! Pa held the bag in one hand and my hand in his other so I wouldn't bounce away or get lost in the crowd. We then stopped at a small beverage cart and grabbed a beer for Pa and a soda for me before finally making our way to our seats.

We walked through a short cement corridor before passing through double doors, where an attendant promptly greeted us. This attendant checked our tickets and pointed us toward our seats. I took this moment to take in my surroundings. Rows and rows were filled with seats, and people went extremely high, to a level that felt like touching the roof. Then, in the opposite direction, people were walking all the way down to the ground court level. There were even more people walking up and down the stairs, selling concession stand items from trays that hung around their bellies or off what seemed like an extremely tall stick stacked with bags of popcorn, cotton candy, pretzels, and more! Others walked around selling more merch, like balloons and light-up toys. The circus wasn't gonna miss a sale opportunity if they could help it.

Once we were in our seats, the lights turned down low, signifying that the show was about to begin. All across the arena, every light-up toy and glowstick illuminated the venue. Pa took the queue and handed me my new scepter; I proudly lifted my scepter, pushed the button, and waved my light in solidarity. Not every person in the stadium had a light, but I did.

Halfway through the show, I enjoyed myself so much that I wanted more. I turned to my dad and said, "Pa, I'm hungry."

Children have no concept of money. We don't know the value of money, how it's earned, and that our parents don't have an infinite amount.

"Okay, mija, we'll grab something in a little bit," Pa replied.

A few moments later, my dad asked to see my new toy, so I willingly handed it over so he could play with it and quickly forgot he had it because I was so enthralled with the show. Horses, tigers, bears, elephants, acrobatics, fire, and more!

Suddenly, Pa pops up out of his seat, instructs me to stay in my seat, and says he'll be right back. He swiftly returned, and he brought me nachos! I immediately began eating. After devouring every chip and cheese drop, I remembered my toy and asked, "Pa, where's my toy?"

"Ay, mija, I left it in the restroom! I'm so sorry!"

I immediately pictured my dad walking into the restroom and setting down my toy on the counter so he can pee, then washing his hands and walking straight out. Pa was a good actor. He could have sold a used car to a used car salesman.

That's the last thing I can remember from that night. When I was older and looked back on that memory, I understood that my dad must've returned the toy to have money to buy me food. But would they take returns? He may have had to sell it to someone else to make the money back to purchase the nachos.

Why did I have to be so greedy? Did I cause my dad to feel guilt or shame for not being able to afford both?

I could have enjoyed the toy longer than the five minutes of consuming nachos. I wish I knew then what I know now. I try to assuage myself by remembering the fact that I have zero toys from my childhood remaining in my possession. But, it doesn't give me any relief on how I could have possibly triggered my father into feeling less than.

Home Sweet Home

It was summer break, and I was staying with my dad for several days. The weather had been hot and sunny. This summer, Pa was sober and renting his own apartment in North Houston off West Little York. I had a bag packed with a few days worth of clothes, my toothbrush, and other necessities. I had packed one of my favorite outfits; it was a thin, sheer top with a colorful fruit pattern featuring watermelon, strawberries, bananas, and I had a somewhat matching ruffle skirt to pair it with. The print scheme made me happy, and it was perfect for that time of year.

Pa borrowed a car to pick me up, and we listened to his favorite bands: The Cars, The Eagles, The Rolling Stones, etc. The original "dad rock." We headed over to visit Tía Sonia's apartment, where we also visited my other aunts, uncles, and cousins. Three of my dad's sisters all lived in the same small apartment complex. Lovely for my cousins because they had each other for playmates and grew up together. I'm sure my dad's siblings also appreciated having each other close by for support or at least the comfort of proximity. I'm also sure it caused a lot of friction. Can you imagine living next door to your siblings?

Later that afternoon, Tío Jesse drove Pa and me back to his new place. I remember reading the green street sign after exiting the freeway and before we made a right off the feeder road. A short distance later, Tío Jesse made another right into an apartment complex I had never been to.

For the most part, my close and extended family lived in the same neighborhood for as long as I could remember, so traveling an entire freeway to another side of town I didn't recognize felt odd and out of place. Why did Pa choose to live so far away from the family?

We exited the vehicle, thanked my uncle for the ride, and reminded him to drive safely back, waving goodbye as he pulled away. Pa grabbed my bag, and he guided me up the concrete stairwell with metal railings covered in a shiny black paint coating, which had been chipping off in thin wispy flakes in areas worn down by everyone's touch, revealing the rust underneath. At the next landing, Pa stopped at a green door finished with a fine coating of dust, bare of a welcome mat. Pa pulled out his copper colored key. I noticed he had no other keys accompanying this one on the ring, but it made sense since he didn't have a car or any other properties. Pa inserted the key into the deadbolt, twisted it, and with the opposite hand, still holding the straps of my overnight bag hanging in his palm, grabbed and turned the knob.

The door swung open, and Pa gestured with an outstretched arm for me to walk in first. I first noticed the scent. The apartment I lived in with Mom and Erica smelled different. Here, it smelled like fresh paint, which to me meant it was a clean apartment. Light brown carpet, bare white walls, a large living room window with thin white blinds partly opened, inviting sunlight to brighten the space, and a counter bar cut into the kitchen wall.

I took several steps inside until I was standing in the center of the unfurnished living room. To assess the size of the space, I looked up to find where the walls and ceiling met. It was so spacious, like a blank canvas. Bringing my arms up and out like a "T," I spun around in circles to take advantage and fill the space with my energy. This is where

I would stay with Pa. We could finally decorate a place however we wanted and make it our own. Our home. He never stayed in any other apartment long enough to give us that opportunity.

Pa smiled; he saw and felt my joy. Maybe he was thinking the same thing I was.

Pa walked to the other side of the unit, towards a set of doors, and I followed. He walked through the right doorway, and I saw two beds—one on either side of a single, centered window. I had my own bed! The mattresses were on the floor instead of bed frames, but that was okay; I didn't mind. I could sleep anywhere and on anything. I run in from behind Pa and jumped on the nearest mattress. It was fitted with covers and a pillow, waiting for me to crawl in, cover myself, and drown in dreams.

I quickly settled on the bed to assess the rest of the space and saw a small TV on a nightstand in the opposite corner. I glanced up and found a ceiling fan. Pa followed my eyes and flipped the switch to turn on the fan, and the light bulb switched on simultaneously. Pa set my bag down beside the bed and ordered me to unpack. Happily, I pulled out my toothbrush, hairbrush, and clothes. I stand holding everything in my arms, and Pa opened a second door from inside the bedroom that led to another space.

This half-room had a sink and a small counter with a mirror. It smelled like Irish Spring soap. I found the scent's origin. Pa had a bar of soap set on the sink, and I was certain I would find another bar in the shower.

I put my toothbrush in the same plastic cup as Pa had his in, and I placed my hairbrush beside his comb. I picked up my clothes to find the closet. It was a nice-sized walk-in closet, but there were very few articles of clothing hanging, leaving the majority of the hanging rods empty and bare. Apart from the clothes, Pa only owned one other pair of shoes: his rugged, worn, paint-stained work boots. I set my meager pile on one of the empty built-in shelves. I walked out of the closet and see the toilet and shower had a private space, complete with a door. This was good because if one of us was in the shower or using the restroom, the other person could be at the sink in front of the mirror getting ready. Or, you could close all the doors and have the whole space to yourself.

Pa asked me if I was thirsty or if I wanted a snack. Uhm, yes! What kid is gonna turn down a snack? He turned towards the kitchen, and I followed.

Dark walnut brown cabinets line a narrow, galley-style kitchen with white appliances and a stainless steel sink. Pa opened the pantry closet and pulled out a package of Oreos. He asked me if I wanted milk, but I shook my head no in disgust. I didn't like to drink milk; he should know that. But he suggested I use the milk to dunk my Oreo cookies, and he was right. Turns out I like soaking my Oreos in cold milk until soggy and then feeding myself the sweet mushy goodness. He poured me a short glass of milk. Since the apartment was unfurnished, Pa told me I could eat in the "room," as in the bedroom. So back to the room I went. Pa turned on the TV and began flipping channels. I dunked my first Oreo until my index finger and thumb came in contact with the ice-cold milk. This cookie was gonna be so good. Life felt good.

That night, Pa and I walked several blocks to a nearby Taqueria Arandas. Back in the 90s, taquerias had large, colorful, and fun street art on the front windows depicting huge tacos, tortas, sopas, and aquas frescas. Personally, that's how I judged if the food would be good or not; if the art made the near cartoon-style food make you hungry and crave a dish, then the food promised to be good, especially if the depictions showed avocado in them!

We walked in and over to a booth to seat ourselves. The booth had the hard, curved-style laminate wood bench seats with bolts in them. Using my knees, I crawled into one side, and Pa sat across from me. From my seat, I could see the trompo, which was the marinated pork to make tacos al pastor on the vertical pit rotating and sweating savory juices. The taquero took their long knife and made several swift slices, catching the chopped meat in a tortilla held by the opposite hand. The mesera walked up and offered us menus, then asked, "Que le gustarian tomar?"

You don't have to speak Spanish to know the queue. Waitresses always take your drink order first. I told Pa I wanted Cola Champagne, but they don't serve the Salvadorean soda at Mexican taquerias, and he asked if I wanted another drink.

"Can I have a lemonade?" I asked. Pa nodded his head and looked at the waitress, who was already taking note of my Limonada order, and Pa ordered himself a cerveza.

"What do you want to eat?" Pa asked.

"Two tacos," I responded.

I really should have elaborated on what kind of tacos I wanted and with what toppings, because what arrived wasn't what I had in mind. Children assume parents can read minds and or automatically know our likes and dislikes. The tacos I received were on the dislike list.

The mesera sets my red plastic taco basket in front of me, and I thought that there must be been some confusion. On the tray were two flour tortillas with some sort of meat completely covered in cilantro and onion. I looked up at Pa, who read my face. He picked up the salt shaker and gave a few shakes over my tacos. I also don't like my food overly salty, but Pa was a salt addict. Often, he would pour salt into the palm of his hand and eat it, dry!

He picked up the taco, folded it in his hand, and handed it to me. I took the taco with my hand and held it over my plate.

"Eat it," he said, with a "trust me" tone.

I looked down and took the world's tiniest bite. I tasted salt and onion. I spit out the onion. Pa picked up my plate and, with his fingers, started removing the heavy-handed cebolla from my two Barbacoa tacos.

I slowly picked at the tacos. They were fatty, and if I chewed on fat, I would gag and throw up. Thankfully, the tacos had a slice of avocado on each, so I happily eat that. The were very thin slices of avocado, so thin they were nearly translucent. I picked at my tortilla because the flour absorbed the flavor of the meat. Pa looked disappointed when I stopped eating, and he asked the mesera for a to-go box. Pa paid the bill, and we made our way back to the apartment.

When we got back, I changed into my sleeping clothes, brushed my teeth as he instructed, and when I was done, I crawled into the same bed he was lying on to snuggle. After watching TV for some time, I began to feel sleepy. I snuggled into his side with my face on his chest while he continued watching TV. That was my favorite way to sleep. In his arms, head on his chest, listening to his heartbeat, feeling safe. A girl's dad is her protector, and I knew Pa would protect me against the world.

Pa found the Saturday cartoons to keep me entertained while he showered and dressed for the day. I set the now bowl of milk on the carpeted floor and scooted back into bed and under the covers. Just then, Pa opened the door and told me it was my turn. I got up and headed into the shower.

What do you know, that familiar green lightly marbled bar of Irish Spring sat on the built-in ceramic soap caddy. I smelled it before I saw it. Once I was out of the shower, Pa yelled for me to brush my teeth. I liked that he would remind me to brush my teeth because I never did at Mom's place. And I liked that Pa would have me brush after I ate breakfast. That made so much more sense.

After I dressed, Pa then reminded me to brush my hair. I had long hair that would tangle, so I typically avoided doing so. At home, Erica would take care of my hair. It hurt when she put my hair in a ponytail because she would pull it back so tight, and sometimes, the hair tie with the two plastic balls on the end would pop and hit my head. Or the tangles in my hair would have to be combed out, and that would yank the hair at the root, leaving my head and scalp tender. But Pa didn't like me to leave the house looking like a mophead, or despeinada as you would say in Spanish, so I had to do my best.

He locked the front door, and we headed down the stairs. It was a hot and sunny day. We walked east, down West Little York, with each step feeling heavier. I imagined the soles of my shoes melting into the pavement. The sun was beaming and absorbed into each strand of my dark hair, baking my scalp. The top of my head was so hot, you could have placed a cast-iron on top to bake a Salvadoran quesadilla. Even with the heat, Pa and I kept a firm grasp, holding each other's hands as he walked on the outside of the sidewalks, nearest traffic. After what felt like half a day, we made it to the shopping center and walked into a Payless Shoe Store.

Once inside, he released my hand, and the cool, air-conditioned temperature immediately made contact with my palm, making it feel colder than the rest of my body, much like holding onto melting ice.

Pa called for assistance and had an associate measure my foot to ensure we tried on the right-sized shoes. I removed my shoes and set my right foot into the silver contraption that expanded, then moved inward to pinpoint my shoe size number. Pa then began pulling a few boxes with shoes inside for me to try on.

One pair was white sneakers with all the fun girly colors, and they lit up! I ran up and down the aisle to test them out. Another pair was camel-colored ankle-high boots with dark brown faux leather at

48

the top, rugged-style laces, and a thick rubber-like sole featuring a slight heel. These were very popular in the 90s, resembling hiking or construction boots. If you're familiar with the popular Timberland boots, then you know what I mean.

Pa had me take a couple of steps here and there, then I admired my reflection posing with them, and we both decided these would be the shoes he bought me. We walk out of the store pleased with our purchase.

Later that week, we got ready to go visit my Tías, and Pa reminded me to wear my new boots. I ran over to the bag to remove the box and sat down. Pa helped me remove the large wadded-up paper set inside the shoes to hold the shape, and he adjusted the laces. We put one boot on at a time, and he laced me up. He gave me an approving nod, then off we went.

During our walk to the nearest Metro stop, I began to feel a prick on the back of my left ankle. I tried to ignore it, but when we were seated on the bus, I told Pa the back of my foot was hurting. He told me he would look at it once we got to Tía Estella's. The discomfort grew even worse when we exited the bus and began another walk. He told me I had to keep walking. Each step felt like someone was taking a razor and slicing my Achilles! On both feet, nonetheless. I tried walking like Frankenstein to help alleviate the contact, but could only do it for so long. I sensed a shift, and could tell Pa was frustrated by his tense body language. I didn't want him upset with me, so I had to try to force myself to walk as normally as I could.

When we finally reached Tía Estella's apartment, we immediately removed my shoes only to find blisters, rubbed raw and peeled, on the back of both ankles. Pa sat at the dining table, speaking to Tía Estella in Spanish while they each inspected my brand-new boots. I couldn't understand what they were saying, but when I looked over at him, I could read both disappointment and frustration on his face. I felt so guilty, like I had done something wrong. I knew Pa had spent his hard-earned money on the shoes, and they wouldn't be eligible for an exchange since I had already worn them out. So they planned to give the shoes away to someone else.

A part of me thinks the blisters and discomfort had to have been caused by the socks I wore. The day I tried on the shoes, I wore a thin pair of socks, but that day, I wore thicker socks. Also, they measured my right foot in the store, but my left foot has always been slightly bigger. Or, maybe I had blisters because the boots weren't laced up properly.

During my continued stay with Pa, the work week arrived, and he had to return to the body shop. Since it was just the two of us, I had to stay in the apartment solo. In the mornings, Pa would wake me after he got ready for work, fed me, and ensured I brushed my teeth. He would turn the TV on and before leaving, let me know he would be back home for lunch. I spent the mornings lying in bed, watching cartoons, playing with my toys, or coloring the pages of my new activity book.

One morning, Pa mentioned it was nice weather and opened the bedroom window. He warned me not to lean out of the window too far because I would fall out and injure myself, so I promised I would be careful.

Later that afternoon, while I was watching TV and coloring mindlessly, a Snickers bar flew right through the open window and landed on the bedroom floor, seemingly out of nowhere! I was happily surprised, and I rushed to the window to look out and find Pa. My eyes darted left, right, down, and around. I couldn't see Pa anywhere. He was able to toss the candy bar with perfect aim through the window and run off before I could spot him. He was such a trickster. I wonder if he hid behind a tree or a pole to watch my reaction. I hope he did so that he could capture the elated smile on my face.

The following weekend, Pa invited his cousin Fabricio and his daughter Jennifer over for dinner. In preparation, Pa borrowed a folding table and chairs. He moved the TV into the living room and cooked mac and cheese for us picky girls. When Pa served Jennifer and me our bowls, we made our way to the living room to sit down in front of the TV while we ate, while Pa and Fabricio sat at the folded table. At one point, I looked down into my bowl of food to scoop the elbow noodles, and I saw something dark. The first thought that crossed my mind was that it was a large speck of black pepper. But I had never seen someone add black pepper to mac and cheese, and I didn't see other specks of pepper. So I moved a few noodles around to get a better look and quickly realized it was not a pepper flake, but a tiny baby cockroach.

I didn't want to make a scene, so I carefully maneuvered the noodle with the roach over to the edge of the bowl, and though I lost my appetite, I pretended to eat the rest. I kept looking over at Jennifer, hoping she would hurry up and finish eating so that we could take our bowls over to the kitchen at the same time. Maybe then Pa wouldn't notice.

I hoped that when Pa emptied my bowl, he didn't see the tiny roach; I didn't want him to feel embarrassed or ashamed.

On another night, Pa woke me, and in my mind, it felt as though it must have been 1 am. He was in a giddy mood and shared with me that the woman we had passed in the hallway downstairs earlier that day had kissed him.

"I think she loves me," he said excitedly.

What sort of clandestine encounter was this? Why was he outside at night anyway? Was he having a smoke break? He didn't smell like cigarette smoke.

Pa was a very charming ladies' man. I hope he and this random neighbor lady didn't produce any offspring I'm unaware of. My Tía Sonia didn't refer to him as a "pica flor" for nothing. For translation, both in language and euphemism, a pica flor is a hummingbird or a "skirt chaser" in Spanish slang.

After my extended stay with Pa was over, he took me back to Mom's place. That was the last time we had a sleepover in that apartment. It hurt me to know that he was fully capable of being a good, providing, and protective parent, but his demons always got the best of him and robbed us of those precious opportunities.

Happy New Year

Tía Gloria, my father's sister, who introduced him and my mom, made the most delicious Salvadoran tamales. To this day, I compare every tamale I taste to hers. And most pale in comparison.

The flavor and fillings of her tamales were perfection. Chunks of plump white meat chicken, a wedge-cut potato slice perfectly tender, a few chickpeas, and more, all generously filled and tucked inside a wall of steamed, flavorful corn dough called masa wrapped in a banana leaf and foil. Anytime the masa would seep out of the leaf and onto the foil, I laid out the foil to use my tongue to retrieve it. To me, the masa is the best bit, and I refuse to waste any of it.

My dad was residing with his sister, Gloria, and her husband, Moncho. Their rented unit was in the same apartment complex where my two other aunts and their families lived. Tía Gloria's apartment was different than my other aunts' because Tía Gloria had a sliding glass patio door in her dining room, which accessed the parking lot, and the others only had windows with a street view.

It was late evening. Pa and I were settled on a sheet covering the floor, with a blanket laid over our feet up across our laps, and bed pillows supporting our backs as we sat against the sofa. It was New Year's Eve, so we watched fireworks play from the East Coast on the TV, when

Tía Gloria emerged from her bedroom.

She began speaking to Pa in Spanish, which I couldn't interpret. Even if I knew Spanish, her speech was too fast. From what I could comprehend, her body language gave off a negative energy. Her words were terse, her arms strongly crossed, her jaw tight, and her eyebrows lifted contemptuously. The conversation quickly ended, and she stomped back to her room, slamming the door. Happy she was gone, I turned my attention back to the TV, but Pa rose and walked to the kitchen.

When he returned, he had a large black garbage bag that he quickly peeled open and wafted up and down, allowing air to open the bag completely. I remained sitting on the floor, my eyes following his every move as he gathered my things and stuffed them into the bag. When he was done collecting my things, he called for me to get up.

"Make sure we don't leave anything behind. Put it all in the bag," said Pa.

I was trying to process why we were packing my things so late at night. I put on my socks and shoes as he instructed me to, even though I was wearing my pajamas and we were just about to fall asleep in our makeshift bed on the living room floor.

We left the apartment, Pa carrying both my overnight bag and the garbage bag, and walked outside of the complex and onto the sidewalk. He took my right hand, and with his other, he held onto the bags tightly as they lay slung over his shoulder.

We walked North on Alder St. It's a two-way street with no sidewalk once you pass the small apartment complex because it is a commercial and residential area. The opposite side of the street only had a deep

54

grassy ditch. It was quiet and dimly lit by the amber street lights. After walking just a few blocks in silence, we reached Lantern Village, the apartment complex I lived in.

We passed the security guard's shack; the guard looked out, recognized me, and nodded indicating we had permission to pass. Pa knocked on my apartment door but no one was home to answer. It was late, Mom and Erica must have been out to celebrate. I looked up at Pa and wondered, "What now?"

He looked at the next unit and knocked on the neighbor's door. My next-door neighbor was my best friend, Gina Guerra. Gina's mom, Marie, answered.

"Buenas Noches, Señora. I'm sorry it's late. Betty's mom isn't home, and I don't have a place to keep her the night; can she stay with you?" Pa asked Marie in Spanish.

Thankfully, we didn't wake them since it was New Year's Eve; they were still up, as noted by the light shining through their window blinds and the music playing from their speakers.

Marie graciously accepted me into her home. I gave Pa a kiss on the lips and a tight hug before saying goodbye, heartbroken that my time with him was cut short, as usual. Time with my dad was always rare and therefore very precious to me. Head hanging down, I walked into Gina's home, dragging my bags behind me.

Gina ran up to greet me excitedly. "Happy New Year!" she exclaimed, with a party crown on her head and a noise maker blowing out of her mouth.

It hit me; Gina and her family were together celebrating the new year as a family, but my aunt just kicked me out of her home separating me from my dad, and I don't know where my sister or mom were. Although Gina's house was alive with celebratory fun, I felt abandoned and alone. I escaped to the restroom to shed a few tears.

What did I do to deserve that? To pack my things in the middle of the night, forcing me and my dad onto the streets on one of the most dangerous nights of the year because of increased drunk drivers. Who splits up a father and daughter on a holiday?

From then on, I hated having to speak to or even acknowledge Tía Gloria. She was soulless in my eyes.

I was always curious to know how it made my dad feel, but I could never ask him for fear of his getting angry with me for questioning his sister. I wonder what their interaction was like the next day. Did his heart hurt like mine did? Did he feel inadequate or emasculated because he couldn't shelter me that night?

Maybe she kicked me out as a safety precaution. Years later, I learned that her husband allegedly showed a few of my young cousins pornography, so perhaps she knew of his sordid ways and didn't want me in a potential situation where my father would find out. Lord knows that if this were true, and I had been part of the group of girls, my father would have murdered the man.

Priorities

My mom would pick me up after school. Cunningham Elementary was just under a mile away from our new apartment, making it a short ride even in school traffic. But Mom hated having to wake up late in the afternoon and deal with school traffic. She treated it as the worst part of her day, as if it were the most inconvenient task.

During that 3pm hour, several yellow school buses lined up around the block, competing with other family cars and shuttle vans. Driver's were limited to driving under twenty miles per hour. Cross-guards stopped traffic to allow the kids who walked home the opportunity to safely cross the streets, and the school administration attempted to keep traffic flowing by guiding children to their right bus, shuttle, or personal vehicle.

To avoid all of this, my mother would wait forty-five minutes or longer to allow the school traffic to clear out before heading my way. Because of this, I was always the last child in the gym or schoolyard. School staff would approach me and ask me where my parent was. For reasons I can't explain, their questions always felt like an interrogation and would trigger me into an emotional spiral.

Did my mother forget me? Was she in a horrible accident? Was she still asleep? The anxiety would crush me, and I would react in tears. The admin would then walk me back inside the building so I could use the phone inside to call home. Each time I dialed, the house phone would just ring and ring. And if our landline just so happened to be disconnected because we didn't pay the bill, I'd have even more feelings of dread and abandonment in my gut.

Of course, while I was in the admin office calling home, my mom was en route to the school. Walking back outside, we'd find the infamous Camaro. Infamous because all the kids at school recognized my mom's Camaro. It was a special, limited edition, black model which featured carburetors above the hood and a red heartbeat pin-style stripes down either side. The look, the sound, and the appearance of her driving it were memorable and iconic.

I would run to the car, relieved to finally get inside and feel secure again. The school admin would remind my mother of pick-up times, and my mother would shake her head as though she agreed to be on time in the future. Sometimes, she would be upset with *me* for making *her* wait, snapping at me to stop crying and to just wait for her next time.

Once, on our way home from school, I failed to shut the passenger door properly. This was because we were not allowed to slam the car doors shut. Slamming the heavy Camaro door, Mom said, would lead to jostling the interior mechanics, such as the motor to power the window or unalign the hinges. If we accidentally shut the door too hard, she would yell and scream about us mistreating her car.

This car was my mom's prized possession. People would stop her everywhere we went to ask her about it and take pictures. She loved the attention.

We were stopped at a red light at the intersection of Gulfton and Chimney Rock when the car to our right gestured for us to roll down our window. Mom obliged, curious to know what they wanted to say or ask. The driver of that car informed us that my passenger door was

58

ajar. At that exact moment, the traffic light turned green.

Suddenly, Mom wrapped her right arm around my left arm, pulling me in close and tight, then said, "Don't worry; I won't let you fall out."

Surprised by her reaction, I looked up at her face, and this thought immediately entered my mind: "She actually does care about me."

It was the first time in my life I felt proof, or was convinced, that she loved me. I was six years old.

In contrast, I never questioned the love that Erica and Pa had for me. They always treated me as their number one priority, as though I were the most precious girl in the world. In contrast, it felt like Mom was *Mom's* number one priority, and *she* wanted to feel like the most precious girl in the world.

Mom taught herself how to dye her hair and never let her dark roots grow out too long. We would often pop into Sally's Beauty Supply for her to pick up the processor she needed to bleach her roots. Then she would often buy makeup and nail polish at the local Eckerds or Walgreens. My mom cared for her clothes by hand washing them to maintain their delicate quality. This was a stark difference for her lack of care for my clothes, which she made Erica's responsibility. Erica and I would spend weekends at the local washateria where Erica washed our clothes.

Erica helped dress me before school, but by the fifth grade, Erica had moved out. One fifth-grade morning, I woke up late for school. When I looked in the closet, in a panic rush, I couldn't find clean clothes to wear. I quickly scanned the area and found a pair of jean shorts crumpled on the closet floor. I threw them on with a random t-shirt I grabbed, and off I went.

When I walked into class late, all the other students were seated, and my fifth-grade teacher, Mrs. McDaniel, took one look at me and gasped so loud that everyone turned their attention and looked at me.

"Oh no! No, ma'am, you cannot wear that to school!" Mrs. McDaniel scolded through exasperated breaths.

"Let me take a picture of this inappropriate dress," she added while pulling out the camera.

CLICK! FLASH!

The camera my teacher happened to have nearby was due to a grade-wide art project. The students in the fifth-grade class were each loaned a camera and provided a few rolls of film. The art project aimed to introduce students to the world of photography. At the end of the project, a few select students had their photographs printed in large formats and featured in a gallery at a local Houston museum.

I was one of the few lucky students with a photograph on display in the gallery. My photo was a "selfie" featuring my sister, me, and one of our orange tabby kittens with our heads pressed close together like a three-headed monster. I didn't have the opportunity to see my work on display at the museum.

My shame was immortalized on film forever. Why was this necessary? My mind swirled with thoughts and emotions. Mrs. McDaniel was being dramatic and mocking me in front of my peers to make an example out of me. I was angry with her for that. I was one of her top students academically. She hand-picked me to lead group projects, competitions, and so on. I felt as though she was forgetting all of that and betraying me.

I was embarrassed, but I tried to play it off. I rolled my eyes and laughed as if the teacher was the outlandish one.

"Go down to the nurse's office and call your mom to bring you some pants." Mrs. McDaniel ordered.

I dropped my backpack off at my desk, snatched the hall pass from the hangar, attempted to slam the classroom door behind me, and slowly made my way to the nurse's office. The classroom door, unfortunately, had a soft- close feature, so it didn't make the dramatic impact I had hoped for.

At the nurse's office, I explained the reason for my visit. The nurse looked me up and down with judgment before instructing me to knock on the guidance counselor's door for assistance. Why do adults treat children this way?

I then explained to the counselor my purpose for bothering him. He attempted to call my Mom, but no answer. Mom had a habit of turning the phone ringer off or unplugging it entirely during the day so that she could sleep undisturbed.

"You can't return to class without proper attire. Those shorts do not meet the dress code. Your fingertips are way past the hem," he explained.

I didn't respond. I had no other options.

"Let's see if we can find something that will work. You'll have to follow me," he added as he rose from his chair.

I followed him to an annexed building, where he unlocked a closet door and pulled out a large cardboard box. It was filled with Lost & Found items.

"There are some clothes in here you can try to find to wear." He said.

I began to shamefully rummage through the box of old, forgotten clothes. It contained mostly hoodies, but I needed to find an alternative or be sent back home. At the moment, I felt like a homeless person scavenging through a dumpster. I fought back tears.

I found a pair of sweatpants that, thankfully, I could pull over the shorts I was wearing. In the fifth grade, I weighed one hundred and five pounds, the size of a small adult woman, not the average size of a nine-year-old girl, so the odds of finding pants that would fit me were slim.

I quietly thanked the counselor before walking back to class with my head down and trying to hide my shame of wearing a stranger's pants.

"I hope no one peed in these pants," I worried to myself. The shorts I wore already smelled of cigarettes. They were my mother's Daisy Duke cutoff jean shorts that she wore to the cantina the night before. Mom didn't stop me from wearing her shorts to school, so I assumed that meant they were fine. Perhaps it would have been wiser to sleep in and skip school that day rather than show up and be humiliated in front of my entire class.

At this age, I hadn't been taught how to appropriately dress. I had received no lessons on color coordination, choosing clothing articles with similar styles, dressing for my body type, or ensuring clothes were clean and pressed.

Mom's second priority was her car. Her pets were third, and if there was a man in her life, he was fourth, leaving me at the very end of her priority list.

Mom picked up every stray she could get her hands on. At one point, we had two pregnant cats who gave birth in the same week. This led to us having twenty-something cats and kittens in a one-bedroom apartment. Chaos does not even begin to describe it. You know the "crazy cat lady" from *The Simpsons*? I joke that that was my mom.

Kittens were climbing up the curtains and scaling the old school vacuum cleaner that had the cloth bag on the backside which housed the removable plastic trash bag inside. We could hear and feel them crawling underneath the sofas. And the meowing was incessant. To make matters worse, there were only two litter boxes, and they were always filled with filth.

Sometimes, I was the stinky kid at school because a cat would spray urine on my belongings. It could be on my shoes, backpack, or clothes. It would be too late before I would notice the smell outside the house, and that the smell was coming from me. Occasionally, my classmates would make comments about the odor, and I grew self-conscious.

Even though money was tight now that she was a single mom again, Mom only purchased the best for her cats. While I was left to eat cheap instant Maruchan cup noodles or 99-cent Whoppers from Burger King on a daily basis, the cats were treated to a fine mixture of canned tuna and dry kibble, with a side of milk. If I wanted some tuna, I could have some. But I hate tuna. And I hate milk.

The next boyfriend Mom had was a man named William. Initially, I didn't like him coming over to visit my mom. William and Mom would disappear into the bedroom and stay hidden away for hours or the entire night. When my mom would finally reappear, she would be dressed in her negligee.

We were in a one-bedroom apartment. If I needed to use the restroom, I had to knock on the bedroom door for permission to cross through. The lights would be cut off, but I could see their forms embraced under the blankets and noticed his clothing tossed carelessly on the floor.

Once, Gina came over and we played in the dining room. When William showed up, he went straight into the bedroom, which was located right beside the dining table. A few moments later, I could hear my mother moaning. I was mortified. I ran to turn the TV volume up to help drown out the noise and invited Gina to join me in the living room. Then, I was furious. I felt so disrespected.

Mom and William dated for a while, and eventually, I came to like William because he began spending more time with me. We shared meals, watched TV together, and so on. He even let me play with his hair.

William sat patiently and was a good sport about my accidentally yanking his tangles with the comb. I took the dark, thick, kinky curls, and carefully and methodically placed them in bows, clips, or added accessories that worked with the length. I started to trust him.

Mom left to shop at Kroger's one afternoon, leaving William and me home alone. I was lying on Mom's bed watching TV, and William lay beside me. He began tickling me, and soon we were both laughing and wrestling. He pinned me down, and he quickly bit down on my left breast, then quickly bit the right one.

The first one caught me off guard, and I couldn't process my thoughts quickly enough, but when he bit me the second time, I reacted.

"Ouch!" I yelled loudly.

He released me, and I smacked the top of his head with my right hand. It was an automatic reflex. It wasn't a strong hit; more of an awareness slap. Like the way we would chastise the cats for bad behavior.

He continued tickling me. I thought maybe the bites were an accident. As if it were possible that he didn't know what he was doing. So I began to tickle him back.

Then, he bit down on my nipple. He kept his mouth there for a second, but time stopped for me. This time, I felt an awareness in my gut that something was wrong.

"No, I don't like that!" I said as I wiggled away. I quickly hopped off the bed and escaped to the living room, where I stayed, hoping he wouldn't follow me.

Perhaps when I recounted what happened to my Mom, I didn't do a proper job of explaining exactly what had transpired. I was just a little girl. I didn't make myself clear on how it made me feel. Or I left out details. My delivery was too light. Maybe I waited too long to tell her. No cops, no confrontations or fights were had. Eventually, Mom and William broke up.

Years later, I attended a Quinceañera with my best friend, Valeria. She and I were making our way out of the reception hall to find the nearest bathroom when suddenly, William appeared. I stopped dead in my tracks, my guts twisted.

"Remember me?" he asked with a big, wide grin, hands on his hips.
   "Yes," I responded tersely, hoping he'd read between the lines.
   "How is your mom?"
   "Fine."
   "Can you give me her number? The last time I called the phone was disconnected."

I gave him a fake number and walked away. My mood soured for the rest of the evening. Thankfully, that was the last time I ever saw him.

Juvenile

One weekend morning before the start of a new school year, my sister decided we needed back-to-school clothes.

She got us ready to take a trip down to the mall. Before leaving, Erica reheated KFC leftovers from the previous night's takeout. She fixed herself a plate, and I chose to eat a single chicken leg. The fry oil scent came in wafts from the microwave. Once my chicken was cool enough to touch, I began to peel the tasty fried skin. My favorite part of KFC chicken was the salted, yummy, crunchy skin. The once crispy leg, alas, was more soggy than crispy. But it held the flavor. Once I picked at it enough to satisfy my sister's contentment, it was time to head out.

We arrived at Sharpstown Mall and walked in, already holding a large shopping bag, almost as if we were going to return recently purchased items. We began perusing stores, walking up and down the aisles. Some stores we stayed in longer, checking out every corner, searching for nooks and crannies, like we were on a treasure hunt.

In stores that housed circular racks with long dresses, we would play a game like hide and seek. In this version, I would crawl inside the circular clothes rack and cover myself with the clothes so that I was hidden; my sister, standing on the outside, would pick an article of clothing, set it on the rack, and shake it, signaling to me to do my part.

The second part of the game was to grab the item she shook quickly, take it off the hanger, fold it, and put it into our shopping bag. We played several rounds.

Other times, we would go into a dressing room to try on clothes. In this game, if the clothes fit and look nice, we would fold them up and add them to the bag as if we were planning on buying them. At one point, we approached a perfume counter, and my sister asked the clerk, "Can you hold our bags while we continue shopping?" The store clerk nodded yes and began collecting the bags Erica handed over. "Do you need my receipts?" Erica asked. The clerk shook their head "no" and we went on our way.

After several games of shopping, our new bags began to feel heavy. I also started to feel hungry. That picked-at chicken leg was not holding me over very well.

"I'm hungry. Can we go now?" I asked while picturing us eating at the food court. My favorite stall was Taco Bell. I always ordered a few of their crunchy beef tacos. Beef, lettuce, and tomato on a hard-shell tortilla.

Erica agreed to take me to eat, but said we needed to do one more thing. We walked outside the department store and mall, and she set all the bags down and instructed me to wait. "Stay here, and don't move; I'll be right back," she demanded.

Outside, the walls featured concrete panels. I found a large gap between each panel and squeezed into the space, just for fun. Occasionally, I would poke my head out to glance around and ensure the bags were still there.

After a couple of minutes, I heard the glass doors swing open, then heard a few people talking to each other and a sound over their walkie-talkies. "Where is she?" one of them asked. Curious, I peeked my head back out, and I saw a bald, white man who suddenly turned in my direction and spotted me.

"Are you alone?" he asked me sternly as he approached. I didn't respond. I was scared. This stranger had a stern look on his face, and I didn't know where Erica was. He then squatted down to get on my eye level and asked, "Are these bags yours?" pointing stiffly at the pile of shopping bags.

I was frozen in fear. Why was this angry white man speaking to me? Why were the other people standing back, staring? Who were they? Where is my sister? Sudden pangs in my stomach, and started to ache.

The man stood upright and told me I needed to follow him. The people behind him began collecting the bags, and I began sobbing. One of the women in the group attempted to comfort me and told me my mother was inside. Now, I was even more confused.

As I was escorted back inside, I suddenly heard Erica shouting, "Where is my daughter?!" She then noticed us approaching and saw me. As soon as we locked eyes, I began shrieking. Thank God we found each other! She rushed over and enveloped me in her arms to comfort me. She whispered in my ear, "It's okay."

Next, we were escorted towards the back and into a poorly lit office. Erica and I sat in desk chairs. I was still blubbering away. They began asking questions, but Erica was trying to calm me down. To assist her, a young Black man with a kind tone attempted to distract me by asking me if I liked school. I only nodded my head up and down as a yes. Then he told me I should be a good student, make good grades, and "avoid going down this road." What road? What did he mean by that? Adults talk weird, I thought.

After Erica answered several questions, including confirming that it was not, in fact, her daughter but her younger sister, she called home. During her interrogation, someone else took inventory of all the clothes we had gathered and used their calculator to add up the retail value shown on the tags. There were duplicates of the same items. For example, Erica had taken five Polos of the same pattern.

"Over $1,500 worth of merchandise," they confirmed to the group while holding up the calculator to prove the exact number. Then, there was more chatter among the adults. One of them stopped to look at us and said, "I'm going to have to call the authorities because, at this value, it becomes a misdemeanor. You're going to jail." Jail?!?

The police arrived, and one officer pulled out his handcuffs and reaches for Erica. Fear shot through me. The screams from my mouth were of pure terror. I still didn't understand why this was happening. I wasn't aware of what we had been doing at the time. I was just helping my sister prepare us for school by doing what I was told.

They didn't put anything on my wrists, probably because I was so little and because I was still sobbing hysterically. They escorted us out to the parking lot, where there was a van waiting under the awning. The windows were covered with tiny bars. They assisted Erica in getting into the back since she didn't have full use of her arms to balance herself, and they buckled her in. Next, they had me jump inside and sit beside her. As the van pulled away and began driving, I felt so lost. Although I was with my sister, we were inside a scary white van with strangers being driven God knows where. This is what they teach children to avoid, after all! I felt like we were in real danger. My anxiety continued building in my stomach. I became hysterical. Unable to catch my breath, I began to gag.

Erica struggled to lean away as far as she could; she knew what was coming next. She could only slide so far, given the fact that she was buckled in and her hands are cuffed behind her back. I leaned towards her slightly for comfort, and out it spewed.

"Oh my god," Erica said in a low voice with her eyes shut, biting her lower lip and tilting her head away. Unfortunately, my vomit partially landed on her.

"What did she eat?!" the officer in the passenger seat asked while looking back in disgust. "All she had today was a drum leg," Erica responded.

We arrived at a building, and the cops escorted us inside, where they immediately separated us. A tall, large, busty Black woman called me towards her by curling her index finger. She opened a door, ordered me inside, and followed behind me while holding a clipboard.

"Name?" She asked.
  "Betty Feregrino," I said.
  "Age?"
  "Nine."
  "You're nine and already gonna have a permanent record. Congratulations."

Her sarcastic tone was intended to humiliate me while also attempting to teach me a lesson. But I was innocent. All she succeeded in doing was making me anxious about my future and ashamed for reasons I didn't quite understand.

After I removed my shoes and socks for her to perform an inspection, she led me to a different room. I followed, head hanging down, eyes on the floor.

Here, she instructed me to be seated while she shut the door behind her, leaving me alone. The room was fitted with full floor-to-ceiling windows opposite three concrete walls. The windows were not for an outside view, but an office view, so the staff had full visibility into the cells.

I sat on a grey concrete slab that served as a bench and a bed. Beside this was a steel half-wall that only partially hid a matching stainless-steel toilet. There was no seat on the toilet and no door. Anyone walking by looking through the glass could see you pee. When I looked out the glass wall, there were cubicles and people shuffling about. Their offices were directly in front of this no-privacy room.

I remained locked in this room by myself for what felt like days. I curled into a fetal position on the hard bench and cried, wondering what would happen next and where Erica was. Later, a tall, bald-headed Black man unlocked the door and, with the words, "Come on," moved me to yet another cell filled with several teenage girls.

These girls were more my sister's age. Some were standoffish, preferring to be alone, while others conversed in a small group. The same Black woman from my inspection showed up and called my name again; this time, she escorted me outside the building and towards the parking lot, where there was another van.

The sky was indigo and purple, indicating it was evening. I had no idea where the van would take me next as I sat with hot tears streaming down my cheeks, struggling not to make a sound.

We began driving through a neighborhood I recognized; then, I read the street sign, "Chimney Rock."

"Oh my god, am I going home?!" I hoped and wondered.

But then the van pulled onto a street in front of the infamous "Bad Boys Home," formally known as "Burnett Bayland Home." This facility used to be a psychiatric unit at Harris Country Juvenile Detention Center. Growing up on this block, I used to see children wearing all grey and playing games like volleyball or baseball in the yards. When I would ask about them, I was told those were the bad kids who were in trouble or orphaned, and that's why they were locked behind the tall, barbed-wire gates. My stomach dropped, my heart began beating fast, and my eyes grew large as I sat up ramrod straight. I feared this was where they were taking me.

But the van kept driving and skipped the entrance. Instead, the van made a U-turn at Clarewood Drive. Then, it passed the shopping center with the Flamingo Cantina, where my Mom had once worked, and pulled into the next parking lot in front of a building I didn't recognize.

It was fully dark when I stepped out of the van. I met a clerk seated at the receptionist's desk who checked me in. She then pointed me to a door and told me to wait in there. I followed her direction, and when I walked in, I saw other kids, both boys and girls, of various ages and races.

This group was much more relaxed since this was a common room setting with soft seating, a television, and colors on the walls - a stark contrast to the cement cells and dim lighting. A few kids quickly noticed and approached me to ask about myself. I then asked them how long they had been there. One boy casually replied, "A few months."

My eyes must have popped out of their sockets as my neck and jaw jutted forward! "Months?! How long was my sentence going to be??" I asked myself.

I sat on one end of the sofa, trying to distract myself by watching what was on TV. After a few hours had passed, an adult said, "Alright, kids, it's time for lights out. We have a few supplies, and it's first come, first serve, you know!" Suddenly, there was a mad dash by the group of kids, all leading down the hall to a backroom. I followed because I didn't want to get left behind, and since most of them had been there so long, I figured they knew what they were doing. I was one of the last ones in, and I saw everyone lunging at a pile found on a cot, but I was too late, so I ran and sat on an unclaimed cot. Those who were fast enough to grab something showed off their spoils: "I got a pillow tonight! I got a blanket! I got a sheet!" and so on. I sat on the cot, looking around at the other cots. A few kids wound up sleeping on the floor.

The room didn't divide the boys from the girls, which I thought was odd. As I lay down and tried to settle in, I thought about how strange it was that we all stayed in our street clothes instead of changing into pajamas. But where would we get pajamas? We also didn't get the opportunity to use the restroom to maybe brush our teeth. But again, where would we get the toiletries from? It was apparent that this facility didn't have the means to take care of the kids in their charge since we all didn't have adequate bedding.

Restless, scared, feeling alone, hours into the night, someone called my name. One of the attendees stood in the doorway and motioned for me to follow her. I got off the cot and followed her down the brightly lit hallway towards the front foyer, where I first checked in. As I made it further to the front, I saw my mom! I ran straight toward her and gave her a great big hug. I was so relieved to see someone I knew!

The receptionist said to me, "Goodbye, girl! Stay out of trouble now!"
I looked up at my mom for confirmation that I was leaving, and she said to the lady, "Okay, thank you." As she turned us towards the exit.

73

I couldn't tell if she was upset or indifferent.

Her beloved purple Camaro sat in the parking lot, and I climbed inside. A brown paper bag with the Burger King logo was waiting for me. As mom settled in the driver's seat, she said, "The whopper is cold because I had it in the fridge waiting for you." I reached inside, pulled out the burger, unwrapped it, and took a huge bite! I hadn't realized how hungry I was, probably from all the anxiety and worry. I took huge chunks of bites and swallowed so quickly that I gave myself the hiccups. It was the tastiest, most satisfying cold Whopper I had ever had.

Instead of driving two blocks home, we drove in the opposite direction. We arrived at a building I didn't recognize, and Mom said, "Erica is here." This was her jail.

We walked into the brown building, also equipped with sad fluorescent lighting, and approached the desk set up with bulletproof glass. My mom quickly interacted with the attendant and sat in the waiting area. I eagerly anticipated being reunited with my sister and going back home together. Unfortunately, the air from my balloon was released when we learned that, because Erica's charge was so high, they couldn't allow for her release and that she would be moved to another facility where she would have to remain for three months. I cried for my sister. Three months in those cement jail cells? I was heartbroken for her. We had no choice but to head back home and sleep as though nothing had happened. Erica was left behind.

Erica was only trying to help us get new clothes for school. But she admitted she got too greedy. We didn't have the money, and desperate times call for desperate measures. Three months for a minor seems like a terribly long time in comparison to sentences adults who commit more serious crimes.

While not a stellar student, Erica had a good heart. Whenever she hung out with her friends, she had to bring me along, but ensured I felt included. I watched her and her friends choreograph dances in the living room to the latest hip-hop hits. I stood aside, trying to mimic their routine in hopes of joining them. When they would meet up at the pool, I got to play with her friends, too. One of the cute boys was kind enough to let me ride on his back as he dove into the deep end. I pretended he was a whale or a dolphin, and I was a mermaid. I loved the fun energy and attention when her friends were around, but mostly I was just happy not to be ignored.

Nurse Nancy

Gina and I were playing on the second-floor balcony in front of our neighboring apartments one afternoon when a blonde-haired, blue-eyed white lady approached us.

"Hi, girls! Having fun?" the lady asked us.

"Yes," we responded in unison.

"Do you girls want some pop and some treats?"

Gina and I glanced at each other. You're not supposed to take candy from strangers, but this was a pretty woman, and she was a neighbor who would wave hello to our families, so technically, she was not a total stranger.

"Okay," I replied, shrugging my shoulders.

"I'll bring some things out," she said as she turned a heel to head back into her apartment.

Moments later, she reappeared, hugging a basket to her chest and holding it with both hands. It looked a little heavy and was nearly overflowing. My eyebrows lifted high up with curiosity. "Wow, that looks like a lot of treats!" I thought to myself.

"I brought you girls an assortment of goodies. Grab as much as you want!" she excitedly announced as she approached.

Gina and I stood up to inspect the basket of goodies. We were pleasantly surprised to find soda cans, baked goods, candy bars, and even beauty accessories.

"Thank you!" Gina said sincerely.

"Yeah! Thank you!" I said in agreement.

"I'm Nancy, and I live in that apartment with my husband, Lonnie."

"I'm Betty. I live in that apartment," I said, pointing to my door.

"And this is Gina; she lives there." I motioned to the next door.

"Well, it's nice to meet you girls," Nancy replied.

Nancy was dressed in scrubs and wore a stethoscope around her neck, which was clearly visible since her blonde hair was pinned up.

She had a big, white-toothed smile framed by her bright red painted lips.

Nancy was a nurse at Planned Parenthood, and she loved her job. She was proud to work in an environment where she could support young women in health and sex education.

Gina and I began stopping over for play dates and sleepovers. Nancy was the hostess with the mostess. She would bake us desserts and rent us movies to watch. She genuinely enjoyed our company. Nancy had always wanted children, but sadly, she experienced miscarriages and never had children of her own.

After Gina moved away, I began spending even more time at Nancy's place. Her place felt warm with her southern charm decor, the constant stream of fresh-baked goods, and cable! Nancy would often ask about my school studies and offer to help with my homework. Knowing that she genuinely enjoyed my presence and company made me feel wanted and not like a burden. Mom didn't mind me spending so much time at Nancy's. When Pa met her, he liked her, too. I guess they felt a white nurse lady could have been a positive influence on me.

On a visit to Blockbuster, Nancy pointed out a few educational VHS tapes for me to check out. I wasn't familiar with any of the cartoons featured on the cover, but she made it sound interesting and convincing, so we checked out two from the collection. *Where Do Babies Come From?* was the title of one of the movies. I popped in the first rental after she and Lonnie went in for the night.

It was educational indeed. In Texas, sex education lessons are mostly about hormonal changes and a few facts about menstrual cycles, eggs, and sperm. And you have to submit a signed release form from a parent or guardian.

This video, however, explained everything from sex organs to how they work, to how a baby is conceived and delivered. My mind was blown. But I did appreciate learning about the male and female anatomy. This, in combination with her constant education on the various options of birth control, planted seeds of knowledge that would benefit me in later years.

Nancy and Lonnie decided to buy a condo. Fortunately for me, they chose a place near the apartment. After they moved in, Nancy invited me for a sleepover and said I could invite Gina, too. Nancy picked me up on Friday evening, and we stopped to pick up Gina on the way.

When we arrived at the new condo, Nancy gave us a tour and saved the best for last. My very own guest bedroom!

A full-size bed and TV/VCR combo set were inside. Across from the bedroom was a full bath. I was ecstatic! I never had my own bedroom before. I always shared bedrooms with a family member.

"Can I live here forever?!" I yelled while jumping. Nancy just laughed and confirmed I was always welcome.

Nancy then took me shopping so I could choose my snacks, buy a few trinkets here and there, and even get some new clothes to keep at the new place. She even purchased the entire Barney & Friends bed set! Fitted sheet, flat sheet, comforter, and pillow covers. I loved that the bedroom was designed for me, and I took comfort in knowing it really was *my* room.

One weekend, Gina and I slept over at Nancy's place. On Saturday night, she and Lonnie had an event to attend, so they left Gina and me home alone. Gina and I were miffed because Nancy had promised to take us to WaterWorld, the Six Flags water-themed park located next door to Astroworld. Nancy had season passes and would often use her free guest pass to take us to the theme parks. Nancy had mixed up the dates and promised she would make it up to us the following weekend.

After Nancy and Lonnie left, Gina and I had the grand idea to bring WaterWorld to us. Kids rarely have grand ideas that can be trusted. We changed into our bathing suits, but instead of filling the tub, we headed into the kitchen. We laid down some towels, turned the kitchen faucet on full blast, and used the spray hose to play with water. Soon, we lost track of how much water we had sprayed, and the kitchen floor was flooded. We took advantage of the opportunity and used the linoleum flooring as a Slip & Slide.

After we tired ourselves out, we changed out of our bathing suits, left them in the tub, changed into our pajamas, and went to bed.

When we woke the following morning, Nancy gave us a mouthful about the mess we left and how we potentially damaged the condo. She wanted nothing to do with us and ordered Lonnie to take us home. (She later laughed about it.)

Lonnie kept to himself for the most part. He didn't really interact with me. He didn't care to take on any pseudo-parental role like Nancy had. Nancy and Lonnie argued often. I had the feeling that I was often the subject of their quarrels.

Unfortunately, they could not resolve their issues, so Lonnie asked for a divorce. Nancy shared that Lonnie quickly remarried and fathered children. This broke my heart for Nancy.

After the divorce, Nancy rented space, a sort of back guest house, from Erica's best friend's mom. It was ideal for me because I could visit Nancy and see my sister when she hung out with her friend, Eliza, which was often. I also became friends with Eliza's little brother, Ricky. Their house had a pool, and we lived in that pool all summer long.

Nancy loved Halloween as much as I did. She loved horror movies, costumes, and decor. One year, she dressed me up as a nurse using her clothes and a stethoscope, and she took Gina and me to the Houston Natural Museum of Science for a costume contest. I placed in the contest, and a photo of me was featured in the *Houston Chronicle,* as well as an appearance in a local news segment.

Erica joined Nancy and me to cruise around local neighborhoods. Nancy spotted some holiday lawn decor she liked. She pulled the car over, cut off the lights, and nonchalantly asked us to retrieve the lawn decor. And it began.

We got such a thrill from sneaking onto people's private property under the cloak of night, swiping their incredible Halloween decorations, and sprinting back to the car. Nancy would speed away once we were in. We did this several times until one night, a homeowner caught us red-handed. The woman ran to Nancy's car and confronted her.

"How dare you come on my property and take my things! I'm going to report you!" she threatened.

Erica and I began handing back her things through the window as Nancy just rolled along with laughter and no shame.

Nancy also took me to visit the local public library. I had never visited libraries outside of my schools. This place was fabulous! They even had books with cassette tapes so you could follow along, which I would take on loan to help Gina with her reading skills since she was in a lower grade than I was. I discovered the "Choose Your Own Adventure" type of books. These books are not intended to be read from beginning to end, but to guide you through seemingly random pages or chapters based on a decision you make.

The library would even loan out VHS tapes and baking ware, which Nancy adored. We spent several weekends making trips to the library, and I loved showing off to my teachers that I was reading as an extracurricular activity outside of school.

I didn't grow up in a home that celebrated reading, but books made their way into my life and changed it for the better.

In Kindergarten, my teacher, Mrs. Kelley, gifted each student a Christmas book for the holiday. She inscribed the book with our names and a short, sweet note. I must have read that tiny holiday-themed book a million times.

Mrs. Kelley would often take our class to the library; those were my favorite days. At Sneed Elementary, our library was designed in the center of the school, on a lower-level floor, with no walls, making it an open-air library. They sat us students on the floor, criss-cross applesauce-style, while the librarian sat in front on a chair to read aloud.

Brown Bear, Brown Bear was my favorite. The Hungry Hungry Caterpillar, The Berenstein Bears, Rainbow Fish, and other classics exposed us to the world of make-believe and wonders.

PBS shows also inspired my love of reading. Literature-focused shows like *Sesame Street, Reading Rainbow, Wishbone,* and *Ghostwriter* all inspired me to pick up books and read.

During the fourth grade, one title took over the entire grade, dare I say the entire school, and had a mile-long wait list to check out: *The Stinky Cheese Man and Other Fairly Stupid Tales* by Jon Scieszka. I was shocked to see even the class clown boys reading and enjoying it. With *The Stinky Cheese Man* book, it was suddenly cool to read instead of a nerd's favorite pastime. Visits to the library became exciting for all students, leaving us buzzing with anticipation to arrive and discover new titles.

The *Goosebumps* and *Animorphs* series took up the majority of my loans. In one instance, I checked out a book containing old African folk tales. This book was rich with fantastical myths from all over the continent and the Caribbean, such as Anansi the Trickster Spider. The ancient fables were abundant with philosophical lessons for the reader. It left me to wonder why we only heard European-style stories like the Brothers Grimm and Greek mythology, and not tales from other cultures. It seems like such a missed opportunity on many levels.

In middle school, I discovered the author Lois Duncan. She wrote my favorite young adult novels such as, *Stranger With My Face, Don't Look Behind You, I Know What You Did Last Summer,* and many others. A few of her YA books were even adapted as films.

I checked out a Lois Duncan book every week, but unfortunately, my school didn't own her entire catalog, and I wanted to read more. I asked the librarian for recommendations, and she gave me a few, such as Christopher Pike.

Low Fantasy was another favorite genre. I enjoyed the feeling of disappearing into a world similar to my own but with magic. Worlds where I wasn't familiar with the character's vernacular, helping my own vocabulary to grow, where dishes I had not heard of were being served, where classic books I hadn't read yet were being referenced, where adventures were taking place across landscapes I thought I would most likely never see in real life.

My other childhood best friend, Becky and I enjoyed racing to see who could devour the most books. I tried to read the same books she was so we could discuss them. I wish there had been book clubs for kids then. If they had existed, I was completely unaware.

Pizza Hut's BOOK IT program also incentivized reading. You would track your reading and submit the log to earn a Personal Pan pizza and stickers. I proudly displayed my reward stickers on my notebooks or binders and bragged about the number of free pizzas I had earned. The program marketing worked because I then began asking to order Pizza Hut pizzas.

This may be cliché, but the smell of old books always transports me back to my childhood days in a library. And the sound of thick, plastic clear cover bending when you crack open a book gives me happy chills.

Nancy brought fun and adventure to my childhood. She encouraged me to do well in school. She often treated me with love as if I were her own, and she always remembered my birthday. Like all of us, she had good qualities and bad, but at the end of the day, Nancy was an influential woman who often helped fill a maternal role.

Art Meets Racism

We still had art, music, and other programs to cultivate us when I was in school. One lesson in art class focused on the "D.A.R.E." program. Drug Abuse Resistance Education was an education program that seeks to prevent the use of controlled drugs, membership in gangs, and violent behavior.

Mr. Walker, my fourth-grade art teacher, and was the first Black teacher I ever had. Mr. Walker was an older, well dressed, well-spoken, and well mannered, so I admired and respected him greatly. Because it was an extracurricular class, we only met with him once a week, making time in art class especially precious.

Mr. Walker instructed us to create a mock billboard advertising the D.A.R.E. slogan, "Just Say No." After we turned in our artwork, Mr. Walker chose my art, along with two other students. We didn't know, or perhaps I forgot, the three entries he chose would be submitted to a district-wide contest. I was so shocked and honored.

My billboard featured an exposed needle, a rolled joint with smoke billowing from the end, and other drugs bundled with a "no" symbol atop, the universal red circle with a forty-five-degree diagonal line from upper left to lower right.

I know what you may be thinking, and no, I had never seen any of these drugs in person. Even with a drug-addicted father, I was never exposed to his use. I was only aware of his drug use because of everyone's anecdotes and accusations. I learned about drugs from watching TV. We can thank public television for showing me what to avoid.

The students whose art made it to the district contest were invited to attend a special ceremony, and Mr. Walker would be present to represent our school. I was excited to learn I would see him outside of school and that my family would get to meet him, too. Mr. Walker was a mature intellectual with a calming energy, and I appreciated how he spoke to us students like adults.

My dad was so proud to learn about my art submission and the subsequent ceremony that he took me shopping. I wore a new peach-colored dress to the ceremony, and my sister did my hair. It felt like a red carpet moment. We walked into the venue, and there were several rows filled and a large stage. We were ushered to our seats, and when we came to our row, Mr. Walker waved at me and rose from his seat. I excitedly waved back as I made my way over and greeted him with a hug. I quickly introduced him to my family, and he extended his hand and said hello to each of them. As we settled into our seats, I made my way to sit beside Mr. Walker, but then my dad maneuvered me away so that he sat between us. I didn't think anything of it as it was dimly lit inside, and the program was about to begin.

Another student, one with actual artistic talent, won the contest. I believe this earned them a scholarship, and their entry would go on to be featured in places like an actual billboard ad and the Houston Rodeo art fair.

Mr. Walker invited us to head towards the stage, where a step-and-repeat photo backdrop was set up. We all followed and made our way down. When it was our turn, we gathered in front of the camera.

I wanted to be pictured with Mr. Walker, but my dad squeezed his way between us. He did so in a very unsubtle, aggressive manner. Confused, I looked up at my dad, and he wore a scowl: furrowed brows and clenched jaw. Instantly, I knew my dad didn't want Mr. Walker, a Black man, touching me. I was mortified! I know Mr. Walker sensed my dad's aggression, and I hope his feelings weren't hurt. Mr. Walker kept his respectful attitude, acted as though he didn't notice, and let it roll off his shoulder. After the photo was snapped, we said our goodbyes.

On the drive home, I was stuck in my head, overanalyzing the entire night. Mr. Walker went out of his way to attend this ceremony for me. I don't believe the other two students bothered showing up because I certainly don't remember seeing them. Instead of my father thanking him for being a great art teacher who influenced the world's future and opened up opportunities for me, he looked down on Mr. Walker and disrespected him.

I recalled a time when my dad was driving his little black coupe and began street-racing someone. We were driving down the street and we came to a stop at a red light. I sensed Pa look in my direction, so I looked up at him. He was looking past me with a scowl on his face. Anytime my father grew angry, it was palpable. Using my elbows to prop myself up, I peered out the window; the other car was being driven by a Black man who was also giving off tension. They both revved their engines.

"Fucking motherfucker. Wait you fucking motherfucker. Fucking nigg**," Pa said.

He spat the words out of his mouth like venom. There was so much

86

visceral hate in his speech. He didn't even know the other driver. How could this stranger become an enemy in a matter of seconds?

The light turned green, and Pa shifted gears and fired off. My body was pressed far back into the seat due to inertia. Seconds later, he pulled the steering wheel left and swung the car to turn at the next intersection to prove he won. He was in his twenties then, young and immature.

I loved my dad, but his behavior that night was utterly disappointing. My heart weighed heavy on a night when it should have been soaring.

I'll never understand why my dad behaved this way. We are brown-skinned Central American descendants of Indigenous heritage. When we are in the sun for too long, our skin becomes darker, never lighter. One of the ladies from an old congregation of ours was Dominican and Afro-Latina, and he never treated her differently. What made my dad think less of Black Americans? Did it make him feel better about himself? Was he projecting his insecurities?

Most likely, yes to all of the above. Why else would someone remain so ignorant if not to try to make themselves feel better at the expense of others? For someone who was constantly in and out of church, it wasn't very Christ-like of him. In fact, it was downright hypocritical.

Spelling Bee

Cunningham Elementary put on a spelling bee contest. I was great at spelling because I was an avid reader and read above my grade average, so I was sure to win, right?

The school admins began to host after-school spelling bee study programs, and I signed up. We were given the small yellow spelling bee guide featuring the most common words tested, and we held practice rounds competing against all grades. I noticed kids younger than me participating, which I found odd because I couldn't remember spelling bees from prior years.

We had a rotation of teachers host the after-school study program, and each teacher shared new tips on how to process spelling words that we weren't familiar with. I don't recall anyone teaching Greek root words, not to say that they didn't, only that I don't remember. I didn't study Greek root words until high school English during my junior year.

After weeks of studying from the little yellow book and successful practice runs, the big day had finally arrived. My classmates and I queued up to head to the cafeteria, where the contest was held on stage. My school didn't have an official auditorium; our cafeteria served two purposes. It's where we performed holiday concerts and held award ceremonies, and now the spelling bee contest.

The school janitors had set up the space with rows of chairs for family members and friends to attend. These janitors weren't just school staff; they were our friends. During lunch, they would stop at each table and converse with the students. I remember one guy was of Mexican descent, and the other was younger and Puerto Rican.

The older Mexican fellow asked us kids at the table, "Do you know why the fruit is wet when they serve it to you?"

I looked at my orange, picked it up to inspect it, and realized he was right; it was covered in drops of water.

Before anyone could respond, he quickly answered, "It's because the people who pick the fruit, have to use it to wipe off their sweat!" He then demonstrated using a piece of fruit to run across his brow and fling off the sweat.

"Eewww!" "Yuck!" and gagging noises were heard all across the table. The janitors just laughed. I was horrified because I believed him! Even when they laughed it off, a part of me was worried there was some truth to this. In my mind's eye, I could see rows and rows of men and women working the fields under the hot scorching sun, and sweat perspiring from every pore. I personally believe cafeteria lunches are grotesque, especially in the ghetto or low-income school districts. I experienced many gross meals and even found a clear glove in my hamburger and hair in my mashed potatoes.

The competing students lined up against the exterior walls to sign in and receive their contestant badge. The badges had our contestant number typed in large, dark font, and the card was string-tied so you could hang it over your neck to display across your chest. This ensured it was visible to the judges and the audience. My number was somewhere in the three digits, which made me wonder how many contestants there were. Suddenly, my awareness of the number of students and the number of older, potentially smarter students heightened. Now, I was nervous, and my confidence slowly evaporated.

To distract myself, I looked around the audience and spotted my sister! My number one supporter and biggest fan. My heart soared. Next to my sister was my neighbor, unofficial nanny, and friend, Nancy, who even brought her boyfriend, James! Nancy had something in her hands, and when she noticed I was looking in their direction, she waved me down and smiled that bright, big, white-toothed, beautiful smile. The bright, glossy pink lipstick, near-matching blush, big blue made-up eyes, and teased blonde hair stood out in the crowd of mostly brown skinned Hispanic folks. I was given permission to walk over, and she presented me with a bouquet of colorful flowers! I'm sure this was the first time I'd ever been given flowers. I thanked her and returned them to her to hold for me while I competed.

We all waited in the queue for the kid in front of us to be tested and either pass or fail. It's intense. Intense, I-N-T-E-N-S-E, intense. All eyes are on you, and it's so quiet you can hear a pin drop. Even the audience holds its breath. The judges call your name, and you walk up to the microphone, alone, center stage, facing the judges and audiences, and wait.

"Your word is _____," says Judge 1.

Your next move is to repeat the word, spell it out, repeat the word again, and wait for the judge to respond with, "That is correct" or "That is incorrect." Or, if you're unfamiliar, and in my opinion, trying to buy time, you can ask the judges for the following:

- Use the word in a sentence
- The definition
- Alternate pronunciation(s)
- Parts of speech

You either know 100 percent that you were correct or that you tried your best. You win some, you lose some.

I advanced several rounds, and so the number of contestants dwindled. My confidence and nerves were on either end of a teeter-totter. One would be up and then the other down, then they'd switch. This corresponded with the time I passed onto the next round and how close in the queue I was to return to the side stage. I was next in line and was then called to the stage.

"Your word is... avocado," said Judge 3.

Avocado, this is great! It's one of my favorite foods in the whole world! You know that question people ask you, "If you could eat one thing for the rest of your life, what would it be?" AVOCADO! "If you could bring one thing to a deserted island, what would it be?" AN AVOCADO TREE! I've loved avocados ever since my dad wrapped slices up in a warm corn tortilla with a bit of salt sprinkled on top and fed it to me. It was the most delicious thing I'd ever eaten. Even better than chocolate! It's like butter, but better! Actually, if I'm being completely honest, eggs are genuinely my favorite food, but avocado is a very close second! I eat eggs and avocado daily.

"Av-ah-cado, A-V-A-C-A-D-O, av-ah-cado." I said proudly.

"That is incorrect, thank you for participating," said Judge 3.

Hot-white lightning jolted through my body, and a burning lead stone dropped into my stomach. I could not believe it. I had eliminated myself by misspelling my favorite food?! How could I make that mistake? I was sounding it out phonetically in my head, but pronouncing it wrong, instead of seeing the word in my mind's eye. I let myself down. I held back tears of disappointment, embarrassment, and anger as I walked over to the row where Erica, Nancy, and James were seated. They greeted me with open arms, told me how proud they were of me, and congratulated me for making it as far as I did.

After that round ended, the three judges huddled together in whispers. They stood up and looked around the cafeteria. One by one, they began pointing at contestants and calling them back to compete. I didn't quite understand why select students were getting a second opportunity, but then I quickly became excited and sat up straight because this meant I would get another chance.

One judge made direct eye contact with me, "This is it. I'm going to get another shot!" A half-second passed, and she looked away, pointing and calling up another student. My heart sank into a deep pool of disappointment once again.

Why didn't she call on me? Other students chosen hadn't even made it as far as I had! How could she skip over me? "Cunningham Elementary, this contest was fixed!" I thought. "You're not supposed to give students a second opportunity and moreover, you shouldn't skip students who actually deserved it."

When the National Spelling Bee hit the airwaves, I sat down to watch, my study book beside me. It's probably safe to say that at age nine, I would not have made it outside my city or state to reach the national level. Those kids are borderline geniuses. Some of those words are ridiculous. R-I-D-I-C.... well, you get the point.

Mischievous

In 1996, when I was eleven, my dad got clean and sober. My mom allowed him to move in with us in our apartment. Mom, Erica, baby niece Mona, me, and now Pa, all squeezed into a two bedroom apartment. My parents weren't back together as a couple or anything romantic; it was a platonic roommate situation. I think my mother allowed him to live with us more for my benefit than for his. I cried for my dad often and would frequently asked my mom or sister to drive me around, hoping we'd find him somewhere on the streets, proving he was at least alive. Mom knew I yearned for my father's presence in my daily life.

It was nearly October, and Pa had come across a fake plastic or latex foot with phony blood painted on for a touch of realism. You know, the kind you see hanging outside a car trunk or dangling from a plastic chain from a ceiling during that spooky time of year. I still don't know how he came across the faux appendage, but he would go on to use it to the best of his ability. And for him, that meant a prank.

Pa decided to hide the "foot" underneath Erica's bed. She and Mona weren't home yet, so the prank befell her. He coerced my mom and me to play along.

My dad acted angrily when Erica and baby Mona arrived home later that evening. He set his face with a tight jaw, lips terse, and furrowed brows. As soon as Erica settled in, Pa raised his voice at her, accusing her of not properly cleaning up after the baby and leaving dirty diapers under the bed, causing the entire apartment to stink. He continued to act repulsed and frustrated.

My sister was dumbfounded and retorted that she had never left a soiled diaper behind. Pa raised his voice louder than before, seeming even more intimidating and angry; he demanded that she inspect the bedroom and commanded me to help her search for the dirty diapers. Erica left the baby cradled in Mom's arms and begrudgingly stomped off from the living room to inspect the bedroom. I trailed behind her.

Once inside the bedroom, my sister flicked on the light, then immediately dropped to all fours to check under the bed. Using her right hand and supporting her upper body with her left, she lifted the blanket, sheet, and bed skirt for a clearer view underneath. I positioned myself beside her and switched on the flashlight I had handy.

The lumen weren't as strong as we had hoped, giving off a faint amber color. I aimed the light into one far corner underneath the bed, sticking my arm as far back as possible to help illuminate where I could; then, I moved the light into another corner while my sister reached around.

Erica screeched at the top of her lungs and, with cat-like reflexes, shot up onto her feet and out of the room as fast as lighting, and in tears! I immediately followed, laughing obnoxiously as my little-sister duty required, implying I was in on it the whole time.

We all laughed at her in the living room while she was hyperventilated.

When Erica saw the foot, she automatically assumed Pa had killed a man and hid the body under her bed, and that he would surely end up in prison for life.

I had to retrieve the fake foot to show her it was made of plastic so she would calm down. Once she realized it was manufactured, she laughed through her flushed tear-filled eyes, accepting that my dad had not hidden a dead corpse. She was upset with us only for a little while, making the prank even richer.

Before this sober stint, Pa stopped into Foodarama, a Latin-focused grocery store, one that his sister, Sonia, was employed at, nonetheless, and thought it would be easy to steal a few cases of beer.

When he began to bolt out without paying, he was chased by security. He reached the fence behind the store and climbed over to escape. He miscalculated the height of the drop, and when he landed, he severely injured both of his knees.

Now incapacitated, he was easily arrested by the police. Eventually, they had to transfer him to a local hospital for medical care. When a perpetrator is in police custody and hospitalized, they are cuffed to the bed rails with an on-duty officer seated on the outside of the entrance to their room so that they remain in custody and return to jail to proceed with their sentencing, court appearances, etc. Somehow, Pa escaped.

During one holiday season, while living on the streets, addicted to drugs, and without a dollar to his name, Pa resorted to his old tactics of thieving. My father visited the local neighborhood Fiesta Mercado at Hillcroft and Bellaire. He made out with a few faux leather jackets from one of the front apparel shops. He may have sold some of the jackets for cash, traded for drugs, alcohol, or a combination, but he kept one special for someone else.

Pa showed up at his sister Sonia's apartment and handed his brother-in-law, Jesse, a gift. My uncle unwrapped the box and pulled out a beautiful jacket. Jesse inspected his newly gifted outerwear. Jesse and Sonia both questioned my dad on how he could afford such a thing; my dad responded with, "Solo me costó un corrido!" Everyone rolled with laughter, including my dad amused with himself. They knew he wasn't joking, and his delivery was impeccable.

His response translates to, "It only cost me a run!"

Another tale of his tomfoolery included him pulling one over on me. I was visiting Erica at her apartment when she needed to run to the store. At this point in her life, she was struggling financially and extremely poor, so every penny counted. She got dressed and asked if I wanted to join her and the baby on the errand. I declined, opting to stay in my pajamas, watching cartoons.

She agreed to leave me behind but made it absolutely clear that I was not to answer the door for anyone.

"Especially if Pa knocks on the door, DO NOT ANSWER. Do you hear me?" she instructed me while pointing a finger in my direction indicating she was serious.

"Yes," I confirmed, shaking my head up and down.

Well, as fate would have it, shortly after she left and locked the door, Pa knocked on her front door. I looked through the peephole and recognized him immediately. My heart dropped into the pit of my belly, my lungs froze, and my muscles tensed, causing my fingers to curl into fists. I slowly backed away from the door, praying he would not hear me.

"Mija, please. Let me in. I need help," he quietly pleaded.

My soul could not ignore my father's plea for help. Of course, I wanted to see my dad, and to help him. So I broke my sister's rule and reached for the lock.

He was so thin. I mean, he was always lean, but he was skin and bones, just extremely underweight. His clothes were hanging off his small frame, and they were covered in dirt and stains. He must have read my face as I took in his appearance.

He laughed off his embarrassment to lighten the mood and gave me a hug.

"Can I take a shower? I haven't showered in three months," he said.

My mind struggled to grasp how someone could go that long without a shower.

"Can you please find me some clothes to wear?" he asked.

Immediately, I ran to the closet to grab my brother-in-law's clothes. A pair of boxers, a shirt, shorts, and socks. When I returned with the pile of clean clothes, Pa was nowhere to be found. I checked the bathroom inside the bedroom and walked back into the kitchen and living room. There was no living or dining room furniture, so we weren't playing hide-and-seek. He was gone. I slowly walked to the front door and locked it. My stomach dropped.

"Oh no. What did he take?!" I asked out loud. I was sure he had stolen something from Erica, but what was it? And how valuable was it? And how angry was she going to be with me?

When Erica returned, I immediately confessed what had happened.

She rolled her eyes and grunted in response, then began searching with concern. Strangely enough, she did not find anything missing. She drove me home after. Later that day, back at her place, she got another knock at the door. It was him again. She opened the door.

Laughing and with a Cheshire cat smile, Pa walked into her apartment and handed her a a tin Fossil box, the kind of box the brand Fossil used to package their watches. This colorful tin box, which easily fits in your hand, had been sitting on the built-in bookshelf between the living room and kitchen.

She understood the reason for his laughter as she took the tin back from him.

"I'm sorry, Mija, I took this from you because I thought it was filled with coins," he admitted.

Erica had filled the box with loose buttons, to replace lost buttons from clothes when necessary. When Pa picked up the box and shook it, he heard rattling and assumed it was filled like a piggy bank. He ran off before checking, and before I could return to catch him.

In this instance, Erica laughed and called him a "crazy old man." But there was a reason why she had warned me so sternly not to let him in. She had been fooled by him once before, too. After he pleaded for her help once, she allowed him inside her apartment. The next thing she knew, he was gone. She immediately began searching for what was missing, only to discover that he had gone through her fridge and stolen a pack of raw pork chops. This was the only food my sister had, and it was supposed to stretch to last her family a while.

Erica was livid! She stormed out of her apartment and hit the streets, searching for my father. She was prepared to physically fight him. Pa had stolen the only food she had to feed her child and herself, and she didn't have money to buy more. Luckily for him, she didn't find him.

She later forgave him, but she would never forget.

Erica may not have been Pa's biological daughter, she was about six years old when he and our mom met, but he was the only father-figure she knew. He acknowledged her as his daughter and that was that.

My father's charisma was one of his most beautiful and loving traits. Pa always made people laugh and had an infectious laugh himself.

Sex Worker?

Mom worked at La Tropicana off Bissonnet and Bellaire, mostly. A traditional cantina, not one of those restaurants with the word thrown in as part of the motif. A cantina is a bar with billiards and music where men can buy drinks for women to keep them company.

The woman's goal is to look desirable enough for a man to offer to buy her drinks. The drinks, such as a bottle of Corona, would cost double the amount, and for each alcoholic beverage sold, the woman ordering would be given a ticket. Each ticket would be worth a few dollars; at the end of the night, you would cash in all your tickets in exchange for money. It's sort of like cashing in all your Chuck E. Cheese tickets for a toy. This type of business is a good way for the bar to drive traffic to its location, increase liquor sales, and have unofficial waitresses.

Mom typically worked from 9 pm or 10 pm to 1 am or 3 am; therefore, she slept through the morning to late afternoon. I'd come home from school after 3 pm, and she would still be asleep, probably hungover. This was most of my childhood.

La cantina is where my love of cumbias formed. The DJ often played cumbia music, merengue, Spanish Rock, and more. The men would spin their evening companions out on the dance floor. Because of this, my mother had fantastic legs. She would wear her miniskirts and tall stiletto heels, tease her bleached blonde hair, and look like the reverse-exotic "Americana."

Typically, children are prohibited from bars because they're not of legal age to drink, but my mom was able to get me in. During one visit, I noticed a boy from my school, named Ivan, was working the DJ booth. When we made eye contact, I gave him a knowing smile. It felt as though we shared this sort of secret, and that he understood when he smiled back with a slight nod. I never shared at school about where my mother worked or what she did for a living, and even though I didn't run in the same cliques as Ivan, that information never escaped my lips, either.

On some occasions, Erica would take me out on the dance floor. Now and then, men would approach and ask me to dance, but Erica would send them packing. Erica wouldn't leave my side the entire night. Mom would often be asked for a dance, then spin and groove across the dance floor, and I admired her. She looked like an 80s video vixen and would stand out from all the other women.

Mom frequented exotic dance wear shops to buy outfits, then taught herself how to alter her clothes to make them sexier by adding more cuts, slits, corset-style backs, hardware, and so on. She was good at it and even taught me the basics of sewing by hand. I practiced a couple of times with clothes for dolls or stuffed animals, but it was no passion of mine.

Inside the cantina, the walls had art made of neon paint. A topless female figure in a martini glass on one wall, coconut palm trees and ocean waves on another, and music symbols near the jukebox, all illuminated by the black lights.

The floors were sticky from an unknown number of spilled drinks. In the 90s, you could still smoke inside of buildings, and a thick fog of cigarette smoke permeated the room. Street vendors would come into the establishment to sell their goods—teddy bears, light-up roses, Polaroid pictures, etc. The men were encouraged to buy their lady friends these gifts. The more money the men spent on the women, the more likely these women would be their companions during their next visit.

Many men had wives and children back in their home country. They were blue-collar laborers: plumbers, carpenters, roofers, landscapers, etc. yet there they were, spending hard-earned money on women they hardly knew.

When Mom had a "good" customer, she would visit them outside the cantina. These men would take us out to dinner, take us shopping, and help pay our bills.

Because of this work, my mom had earned a certain reputation. Once, when I was in the eighth grade, a boy in my class told others that he witnessed my mom go into an apartment full of men, alone. My classmates were gossiping about it, speculating what my mom was doing, calling her a prostitute, all behind my back. Valerie, my best friend at the time, informed me, and she revealed who spread it so that I would have the opportunity to confront him. Only, I never did.

What could I say? What they speculated, well, we could neither prove nor disprove. They'd all seen how short my mom's dresses were on the rare occasions she would come to school. I was mortified. I did not want to bring the subject any more attention and wished it would go away. Why couldn't my mom be a housekeeper or a nanny or have kept working at Burger King? Heck, she was beautiful enough to bag a rich white man and save us from poverty, as I often encouraged her.

I was inclined to believe the kids in my class. Once when she drove us to visit one of her regular customers, she left me in the car to wait, and I began to snoop around. As I poked around her car, I found her clutch and unzipped it. Looking for nothing at all, I found a sealed condom wrapper. On another occasion, I was rummaging around Mom's car and found yet another condom. My mom didn't have a boyfriend at that time, but she spent a lot of time with men, her customers.

When Mom would visit some of her longest-running clients at their home, she would encourage them to drink. The goal was to get them so drunk, they'd be more generous and hand over lots, if not all, their money. On one occasion, Mom would took a man into his room while I sat in the living room with his brother, who was also very drunk. The brother would sit close to me and try to play. He then suddenly reached and grabbed at my vagina. I pushed his arm away, yelled "No!" and crossed my legs. He recoiled like a scolded dog, squeezing his eyes shut and shaking his head left to right, as if he knew his action was wrong.

I kept all of this to myself because I was too embarrassed to bring any of it up. I was scared to reveal the truth. I feared humiliating my mom.

I don't judge my mom for doing what she felt she had to do to survive.

Innocence & Curiosity

I met Rebecca when I was around ten. She went by the pet name Becky. Becky & Betty perfect BFF names, amiright?!

We were only a year apart and loved all the same things. So much so that we bought matching sneakers and cut our hair to the same length. I read all of Becky's books, and she introduced me to new TV shows and movies on the Disney Channel. With that, we also shared the same Hollywood crushes: Jonathan Taylor Thomas, aka JTT, Jonathan Brandis, and all the other pretty blonde, blue-eyed white boys that had photo spreads in Tiger Beat and Bop Magazine in the 90s.

Whenever we would run errands with her mom, Sylvia, and stepdad, Clifford, they would treat her to these teen magazines, and later on, after reading them cover to cover, we would tear out the center folds and hang them on her wall. We would pretend the boys were actually in her room and make up scenes with us conversing with them. Becky and I had pretty active imaginations.

Because Becky was an avid reader, her vocabulary was higher than that of most students I had classes with. And I loved that about her. She even liked horror stories, which was one of my favorite genres. And I don't just mean the *Goosebumps* book. I meant the *Freddy Krueger's Tales of Terror* book series and the like.

Becky had a drastically different home and family life that I enjoyed participating in. We had dinner at the table in the evenings, and her mom cooked well. I walked away with a full belly every time. They even introduced me to new foods such as Frito Pies. Before bed, the four of us would watch Nick at Nite or WWE wrestling together in the living room. I felt like we were a little family.

Once, Becky and her parents took a vacation and asked me to check in on the pets while they were away. I, being a preteen, would have my mom drive me and drop me off so I could clean the litter box, refill the food and water bowls, check the caller ID and answering machine (the old version before voice mail came along), and generally keep an eye on the place.

When they returned, I was chastised for not having done certain things correctly. They were pointing things out left and right. I can't recall precisely what they were upset about, but I felt attacked. In my mind, I followed their directions well enough, so I called my mom to pick me up, and I avoided visiting again until Becky called, begging me to come to a sleepover. When I did, Sylvia and Cliff told me not to worry, "It was no big deal." Maybe they were just tired from their trip, or they felt bad for chasing away their daughter's best friend.

Becky had been born with Juvenile Type 1 Diabetes, a chronic condition in children when the child's pancreas no longer produces insulin, an important hormone. Because of this, early on in our friendship, I was taught to pay close attention to signs that Becky's sugar level was dropping. These signs would manifest with Becky feeling tired, shaky, sweaty, nervous, irritable, confused, or more.

Becky was a respectful child with a calm demeanor. She would never "back-talk" her parents or give snide remarks, so if her behavior changed, we knew it was time to test her sugar levels. Becky always had to have a blood glucose monitor nearby. Whether in her home or out and about, we carried this kit and a cooler with juice and sodas.

These episodes of her blood sugar dropping could occur without a cause or when no one was paying close attention to her eating habits or energy expenditure. Occasionally, she and I would be so lost digging for dinosaur bones, baking in the kitchen, or pretending we were chemists creating a new formula that we would lose track of snack time.

With the blood glucose monitor, Becky had to use an instrument to prick a finger and place a drop of blood onto a test strip for the handheld machine to read. She would either put her freshly pricked finger into her mouth, hoping the saliva would stop the blooding, or add another Band Aid.

Once, I asked Sylvia if I could use the equipment to understand her pain and learn my blood sugar level out of curiosity. Sylvia obliged, and with that, Becky taught me how to change out the needle while Sylvia explained the importance of not sharing needles and how to dispose of used needles properly. I was not prepared for the sharp puncture or the throbbing soreness afterward. While we waited for my results, I wrapped a Band-Aid on my finger, and it may have been too tight because I could feel the rhythm of my heartbeat.

My results showed my blood sugar level was average, healthy, and maybe a little high. Now I could understand and try to relate better to Becky's discomfort.

What I would not be able to try out would be Becky's insulin injections. That was an absolute "no-no" because it was hazardous. But Sylvia taught me how to insert the syringe needle into the insulin bottle, which was kept refrigerated, and how to draw back the plunger so the barrel held a specific prescribed amount of insulin medicinal liquid. Then I would take an alcohol swab, wipe an area of Becky's arm or leg (her choice) to disinfect while pinching between my fingers to create a bulge of fat, quickly yet carefully insert the needle, push down on the plunger with my thumb, pull the needle out, wipe the injection site with a fresh alcohol swab, carefully cap the syringe, apply a Band-Aid if needed, and properly disposed of the syringe.

I felt like I was a significant part of Becky's life, and with that, I guarded her health like it was my own. She was my best friend; I didn't want to see her sick.

In a few instances, Becky's blood sugar would inevitably drop, and we would have to scramble to pour orange juice down her throat. She would have to drink a full glass of this or soda, even when she would fight against it. In this state, Becky was incoherent, shaking, slurring her words, and unable to string together a sentence.

Each time an episode occurred, I would be distressed and frightened. And when she eventually came around and felt better, we would be a bit melancholy, and playtime would become reading time, which took very little energy.

In the summer, we spent most of our time reading YA novels and watching the Disney Channel. Another form of fun activity would be to write fan fiction of the YA Novels and treat them as screenplays to act out.

We would take turns playing the female protagonist and the opposite male love interest.

Occasionally, a scene would call for a kiss. To remain committed to our writing and acting, we devised a way to mimic a kiss without having to touch lips.

We would bring our faces together, touching cheek to cheek. Then, we slowly moved our heads around to emulate couples who make out. We then rolled our tongues on the inside of our own cheek, finding and feeling the pressure from the other. We began to enjoy these moments. It felt good. As close to the real thing as we could get, so we convinced each other to keep playing make-believe and finish the scenes. Eventually, the kissing scenes lasted longer and occurred more frequently.

Because of this, it felt like something we needed to keep hidden between us. I couldn't explain why it felt wrong, but in my heart, mind, and gut, I knew we had to be cautious so that no one would find out. Becky felt the same way, so we decided to "play" out these scenes in her bedroom closet, with the doors shut and in the dark.

Naturally, curiosity grew and unfolded as we began to experiment. After reading our "script," Becky climbed on top of me, and after a few minutes of our version of "kissing," she slowly began to undulate her hips over mine. In the safety of the closed space, cloaked in the dark, the sensation between my legs grew electric and throbbed, wanting more, so I spread my legs open, allowing her to press closer and deepen her pressure, and I matched her rhythm with my body. What do you know, we were dry humping.

From then on, we constantly tried to find time to keep "practicing our scenes." We would make up excuses as to why we needed to go to her room or to try to stay home alone. At some point that summer, we got reckless and sloppy with our private moments.

One night, we were watching TV in Sylvia's room and lying on her bed when we got the urge. Becky rolled on top of me, we began our check-to-cheek kissing, and she began pressing and gyrating her pelvis into mine. Maybe the TV was too loud, or maybe we just got sloppy, but while we were lost in the passion of our make-out session, Sylvia walked in.

"WHAT ARE YOU DOING?!"

We immediately froze, hearts stopped, eyes wide open. Not a second later, Becky leaped off me, and I scrambled off the bed to stand on the floor. Sylvia just stood there, staring at us, hand over her mouth. I had a knot in my gut, my hands fidgeting from nervousness. To fill the awkward silence, Becky began to feed her mom a wrestling story. I soon jumped in, defending our actions and trying to belittle what she had seen in hopes she would buy our story.

"Stop," Sylvia demanded, raising her hand.

We were silent.

"Betty, go to the other room. I need to speak to my daughter in private."

I dreadfully made my way across the room and was a little fearful of walking past Sylvia.

While waiting in Becky's room, I could not stop thinking about Sylvia potentially calling my mom and or Erica. What would they say? Would they punish me? Disown me? How would I answer to this? Dread brewed in the pit of my stomach.

What felt like an eternity later, Sylvia called for me to return to her room.

I was shaking from nerves as I walked in to stand before her. I can't recall everything Sylvia said as she addressed us, but I remember her saying, "You guys are girl and girl, not boy and girl."

After that night, I stopped having sleepovers at Becky's place, and sadly, our friendship slowly dissipated.

When I saw Becky at school, or whenever she reached out to me, I pretended she wasn't interesting enough to be around anymore. I pushed her out of my life because I was too ashamed to show my face at her apartment. Had Sylvia told Cliff what happened? What did he think? Did he hate me now? I was too immature to move past that moment.

I was ashamed of what happened for many years, well into adulthood. To be clear, I was ashamed because we were caught. Not because Becky and I shared a moment in puberty—a natural discovery of our bodies. Albeit too young, I don't believe we're alone in this, and I don't think it's weird or something to be ashamed of now. If anything, it was safer for us to practice and experiment with each other than with boys because that could have led to significant consequences. Now, should we have been dry-humping on her mom's bed? Hell no.

The GREAT Outdoors

Growing up in the inner city, my "outdoor" experiences included the school playground, the local neighborhood parks on Easter, and the occasional visit to Galveston Beach. As far as my recollection goes, everything else occurred in or on concrete. That was until my fifth-grade year.

Biennially, the fifth-grade class of Cunningham Elementary was given the opportunity to attend camp hosted by our local Young Men's Christian Association, also known as the moniker "Y" or, most popular, Y-M-C-A.

Erica shared with me her camp trip experience; she mentioned crying nonstop because she had never been away from home and, therefore, suffered from being homesick. Blood-red shot eyes, no sleep, no eating, and probably dehydration were her lasting memories. This only concerned me slightly because, unlike Erica, I had grown up experiencing sleepovers at different houses. I was excited about this new adventure. It also took place during Halloween!

Students were informed that half of the fifth graders of our school would be attending Camp Cullen, and the other half would attend Camp Olympia; my class would attend the former. The students argued at lunch about which camp was better, not realizing they were practically neighbors sharing the same Trinity River, and retelling their older siblings' anecdotes and lore.

We were given our packing lists and instructions. When the day to depart arrived, my mom dropped me off at school with a duffle bag packed with clothes, toiletries, shoes, and so on. Students and faculty loaded into our school buses. We had such a long drive ahead that I could have sworn we were crossing state lines. My Walkman kept me company with music from my mom's Madonna cassette. Sadly, the batteries died before we made it to camp. Still, the other children were so chatty that I just listened to their conversations while staring out the window, wondering what camp would be like, watching bridges and farms pass by.

Upon arrival, several other buses were unloading with kids I didn't recognize. My teacher, Mrs. McDaniel, caught my attention because she was saying goodbye to my classmates. I walked over to ask why she was giving farewells, and she then informed me that the faculty wouldn't be staying with us.

My anxiety took over. If there were no family, teacher, or principal, who would care for us? She must have read the worry on my face because she introduced me and the class to our Camp Counselor, Jessica. Jessica gathered in a group to formally introduce herself and welcome us to Camp Cullen. She instructed us to ensure we had all our personal items and to follow her for a short hike.

We were led inside a large cabin, and I got a closer look at the students from other schools. I first noticed they were primarily white, while my classmates and I were mostly Black and Hispanic. I wasn't sure if the other kids were going to like us. Suddenly, the camp counselors gathered on stage, music began, and puppets appeared! This was like a

Broadway production in my eyes, and I was excited for the adventure we would embark upon!

After the welcome show, we were led to another cabin. Walking in, we were immediately greeted with the smell of delicious comfort food. Every meal at camp was delicious! I remember telling my camp counselor, "I've noticed that the food served here follows the nutrition pyramid!" I pointed out the foods and where they fit, even dessert! My belly was happy, so I was pleased. We were then taught how to dispose of our food properly. Organic waste had one receptacle, recycling another, trash another, and finally, a place for our trays and silverware. I'm pretty sure this was my first introduction to composting. It made so much sense to me to return food to the earth instead of a landfill.

Because we arrived on Halloween, counselors dressed up as pirates, then came to commandeer the troops and lead us to "the beach." The pretend beach was filled with sand, and a pirate flag hung above. Campers took turns wearing blindfolds and digging for lost treasure. If we found the gold coins, we could eat the chocolate inside. It definitely fit the "trick or treat" Halloween theme we were looking for.

After each camper had a turn and walked away with golden chocolate coins, our counselors gathered us to lead us on the hike to our rest cabins. This was when we learned that the boys' cabin was about two miles down, while the girls' cabins were closer. We waved goodnight to the boys while teasing them for having a longer hike. Jessica then began to teach us camp songs, which were catchy and fun to do together.

When we arrived at our bunks, we had a few minutes to unpack and find our toiletries because it was time for showers. Some girls from the other school were paired in the room with me and my classmates. One girl was full of giggles and seemed super fun to be around. Her name was Meredith. Meredith had big green eyes, a freckled face, adult teeth too big for her child-sized head, and wild, curly strawberry-red hair cut into a bob, giving her a bit of a 'fro.

I changed my shoes into my flip-flops and carried everything in my hands. Walking in thong flip-flops through the night with only a flashlight lighting my way, tripping over stones and tiny twigs, with sand and dirt catching between my toes was no fun. A line was forming for access to the showers, so we waited. The shower curtains were so thin and wispy that they would flap around because of the water pressure. I felt very insecure and didn't want anyone to see my naked form in the shower, so I tried to wet the walls to stick the shower curtain, sort of like a temporary glue.

I turned around to face the water when I noticed an enormous insect. I screamed for my camp counselor to help me. She directed me to try to cover myself with the shower curtain, and then she focused on finding the bug without looking in my direction and quickly shooing the cricket away. It was the biggest cricket I had ever seen!

There were also several daddy-long-leg spiders in the shower stall, but they didn't bother me as much for so long as they didn't move in my direction. I took the quickest shower of my life and got out of there!

Once we were back in our cabin, I noticed Meredith had taken the top bunk, so I took the bottom. She popped her head over, hanging upside down to formally introduce herself. I smiled and introduced myself back to her. She was my new friend.

The following days were filled with adventure. The first for my group was horseback riding. I was a little nervous getting on my horse because I was self-conscious about my weight. Was I too heavy for the horse to carry? I hadn't been on a horse since I rode a pony in a Fiesta parking lot as a small girl.

As I was assisted onto my horse, I swung my leg over the saddle and all of a sudden, "RIPPP!" I had ripped my polyester tracksuit pants. I was forced to wrap my windbreaker jacket around my waist in order to conceal the long tear. Thankfully, my horse was docile and didn't cause me any trouble. The horse directly in front must have had a large meal because it kept dropping poo on the trail, which smelled awful. That was not an enjoyable part, but everything else was, from the landscape and cool breeze to the meditative sways and gallops. Only afterwards, we all realized how the ride left our hips and inner thighs sore.

Next, we had a day of excavating fossils along limestone hill walls. While I wish we had found dinosaur bones, we found mostly fossils of plants and sea creatures. This was followed by canoeing on the lake. Two to a canoe. Unfortunately, my partner was not very coordinated and kept forcing us to row in circles. I grew frustrated and felt it ruined our experience on the water. She wasn't feeling great about it either so we spent the majority of our time attempting to return to shore. The other kids roughhoused and pretended to attempt to flip their canoes, but after stern warnings, they halted. The lake was roped off to keep us in a small, secure area, probably to avoid losing students downriver.

We hiked wooded trails carpeted in fuzzy green moss and shiny pebbles. I came across a beautiful, large egg-shaped stone, but I ultimately left it behind.

In a field, there were tepees set up, and we had the opportunity to sit inside and learn about the construction and use of tepees by the Indigenous people. Outside of the tepees were targets for archery. The archery lessons were short, and I wished I had more time to practice shooting. I felt I could have been good at it.

On another day, another activity, we played a game of tag where teams were broken into omnivores versus carnivores. The game helped teach us about the sensitive ecosystem of that time. Afterwards, we

116

answered questions about the dinosaur species we played.

On the last night of camp, they hosted a campfire. The actual bonfire bloomed in reds, oranges, and yellows. The event was fitted with marshmallows and candied apples. We learned how to melt caramel, stab the apples with a stick, and roll them around the melted candy before letting it cool enough to chomp into. It was a messy but fun activity. They let us stay longer than the normal bedtime curfew, and we gazed at the stars trying to identify and learn the constellations.

On our last morning, we were instructed to pack before breakfast. During chow, we sang our final songs and cheered our last chants, then finished exchanging our contact information with our newfound friends. We hugged, we cried, we waved goodbye.

Teachers, principals, and charter buses fill the parking lot. Mrs. McDaniel saw me crying, my shoulders shaking, and rubbed her long, flat hand in circles across my upper back to console me.

Settled on the bus, seat belts buckled, I continued to cry. I sat towards the front of the bus on the left of the aisle, and Mrs. McDaniel sat right behind the driver's seat. She looked over at me and turned her body around in the seat to face me, "Aww, Betty, you're still crying. Aren't you excited to come home? No? Well, now I'm sad because you would rather be here than at school with me. What about your family? Aren't you excited to go be with them? Oh, you're gonna be alright."

I couldn't stop crying long enough to answer Mrs. McDaniel. The tears, the whimpers, and the shoulder shudders were all clear indications that I never wanted to leave.

I often reflect on my time at Camp Cullen, especially when hiking through parks or kayaking through lakes. I am forever grateful for the opportunity and experiences. And I still remember my favorite camp song...

"I said a boom chicka-boom... valley girl style!"

Awkward

Throughout my childhood and adolescence, I was told that I dressed like a tomboy. My wardrobe consisted primarily of loose or poorly fitted clothing, no frills or lace or bows, just plain and simple pants and shirts. I also didn't wear makeup as early as other girls in my grade did, or bother with learning how to style my hair. I was plain Jane. My mother was very aware of her style choices, dressing very femininely, but that attention to detail was missed when it came to my attire. To be fair, I also enjoyed wearing oversize clothing since it made me feel I could hide my overweight size. I wish I had known then that I wasn't successful.

In middle school, there was a uniform dress code: white top and blue bottoms. It could be a plain white T-shirt, a polo, or a button-down. The bottoms could be blue jeans, khakis, or skirts for girls. For the new school year, I needed to go back-to-school shopping.

My mom picked up one of her customers and drove us to Auchan. Auchan was a popular store located in West Houston near Chinatown; it was a large retailer selling everything from electronics to clothes to groceries. As soon as we walked in, I spotted a table merchandised with Levi's jeans marketed for back-to-school. I walked over and began looking at the options. I grabbed a few to try on, and once I found three pairs that zipped up, I placed them into the basket. Next, I grabbed a pack of extra-large-sized Hanes t-shirts and a pack of generic white socks. We checked out, the guy paid, and my school shopping was done. I was so excited for the first day of school.

Once we were all in homeroom, I noticed all the other girls were wearing cute, fitted bell-bottom jeans or lovely skirts, button-down blouses, and even nicely fitted polos, whereas I was dressed like the boys in my class. I quickly concluded that we shopped at the wrong store and or in the wrong department. In an attempt to fix my style and dress up my pants, I used iron-on patches to enhance the look. I ironed a three-inch by three-inch yellow smiley face patch, popular in the 90s, onto the left back pocket. I received a few compliments from friends, but because of the positive feedback, I began to wear those jeans more often. Some days, I would forget the rotation and wear them back-to-back, and my peers would take notice. Eventually, I got rid of those jeans altogether.

One morning, while getting ready for school, I realized there were no clean bras to wear. All of Mom's bras were heavily padded, decorated with lace or rhinestones, and not comfortable, so I couldn't borrow any of hers. To avoid being late, I just pulled on my jeans and a Hanes white tee.

The moment I walked into homeroom, my friend Geneva rushed over to me with wide eyes and a concerned expression.

"Are you wearing a bra?!" Geneva questioned me in a loud hush.

"Yes," I lied with a face questioning her accusation.

Geneva aggressively rubbed her hand over my shoulders and upper back to feel for bra straps.

"You're NOT wearing a bra, Betty! We can see everything!" she continued.

I had no response. I walked away hunched over and held my Trapper Keeper in front of my chest. I hadn't realized how large my breasts had grown and how visible they were through a white t-shirt.

That night, I told Mom she had to buy me more bras so I would never have to skip wearing bras again.

Around that time, my sister introduced me to JNCO jeans, which were all the rage. She loaned me a pair, and while they were cool to wear, they were uncomfortable. The bottom of the pants' legs picked up a lot of dirt and dust. Wearing them didn't make me any cooler at school.

One evening, we stopped in at Sears. I had never been here before, and as we walked around, I found a table of cute, girlie jeans and asked my mom if I could have a pair. The price wasn't too expensive and to my surprise, she said yes! I grabbed a pair to try on. In the dressing room, I was able to pull them up easily enough, but the zipper and button were more of a challenge. Once I had them on, I checked myself out in the mirror. These jeans made my legs and butt look great. And I even felt they made me look skinny, except for the giant muffin top that was spilling over. I convinced myself to take the jeans and just wear oversize tops.

The next day at school, I strutted through the courtyard towards my friend, Miriam. She noticed me, but confusion set in. She half stood and leaned forward to get a better look and make sure it was me. I smiled in confirmation, grateful for her reaction.

"Oh my God, I didn't know if that was you! You look good!" she said enthusiastically.
I beamed. Maybe now I could fit in with the pretty, cool girls.

At the end of the school day, while waiting for parent pickup, one of my classmates began sharing that she preferred wearing black bras.

"Black is sexy, and it shows through the white tops, which I like," she said with her best attempt at sexy bedroom eyes and voice.

"Now we're supposed to wear fashionable underwear?" I thought to myself. "I can't keep up!"

Valeria, my junior-high best friend, introduced me to Marshall's and TJ Maxx. At these stores, I could purchase more fashionable clothes and shoes at a more affordable price. New shoes also improved my style and confidence, versus wearing Payless or old-man masculine tennis shoes. I did my best to notice and follow trends of what everyone was wearing, but I couldn't afford the designer labels and mostly wore knockoffs.

In an attempt to continue improving my style and beauty, Mom offered to bleach my facial hair. She would tell me the hairs on my face were long and dark, making my skin tone appear even darker than it already was. Wanting to be pretty and seeking her approval, I said yes.

The bleach started to itch on my cheeks. "Mom, it's making me itchy," I said to her with concern.

"Don't take it off yet, that just means it's working." She dismissed.

"Mom, it's starting to burn!" I exclaimed.

"Okay, wash it off in the sink."

The hair that was not so noticeable on my face was now noticeably golden blonde. And underneath, my skin had uneven pale patches in the areas the bleach lay. I wanted to shave my face. But it didn't end there.

"We should bleach your hair." Mom suggested.

When we washed my hair out, and it dried, it was very brassy and orange. The next day at school, my Black choir teacher, Mrs. Gobert, took notice and, in front of the entire class, said "I LIKE your hair! It looks good!"

I was mortified. If my older teacher liked this style of hair, then there was no way it was cool.

My safe space was English period. Mr. Rhodes decorated his classroom to be a warm, inviting space with comfortable chairs, sofas, and toys. He was always up to crazy antics with something hidden up his sleeve. During one lecture, he had a brick in his hand and suddenly tossed it into the crowd of students seated at their desks. It hurled towards my friend Angie, who screamed and held her hands up to protect herself while maneuvering to dodge the blow. When the brick finally came into contact with her, everyone gasped. She looked down at the brick, bent over to inspect it, and began laughing hysterically. It was a prop made of spongy material.

I was on my menstrual cycle, and since I was in the seventh grade, I was only accustomed to wearing pads. As usual, Mr. Rhodes had us in stitches with all his jokes and dry humor. At the end of class, I asked Angie for the usual "spot check" to verify that I hadn't bled through my clothes.

I stood up, and before I could even turn around, Angie's eyes grew wide and her jaw dropped. She was staring right at my crotch. Following her gaze, I dropped my head down, and there was a massive, dark red bloody stain. I immediately untucked my shirt, thankful it was long enough to cover the area, but internally worried that the white cotton shirt would absorb the blood from my soaked jeans. Not to mention, the shirt was a Ralph Lauren button-down that I had borrowed from my brother-in-law… without permission.

I was absolutely mortified and unsure if anyone else had seen. I had to quickly decide whether or not I would try to go to my next class and request a pass to the nurse's office, or if I should go straight to the nurses office. It was also against the school's dress code to have a shirt untucked, so I ultimately decided to head straight to the nurse's office. It was close to Mr. Rhodes' class versus having to journey across the building and up to the second floor.

I quickly made my way over to the nurse's office, hoping not to be caught by a member of the administration, especially since the nurse's office was located next door to the admin office. When it was my turn, I explained my situation to the nurse who looked as though she couldn't care less.

"Where is your hall pass?" Was her response.

"I don't have one. I came right after the bell rang," I explained.

"You can't be here without it. You need to go to your next class and get it before coming back here," she lectured with an insensitive tone.

She had no sympathy for me. I left with my tail tucked between my legs and my head down, making my way to class. When I opened the door to the biology lab, I avoided everyone's eyes as I walked straight towards the teacher with my Trapper Keeper binder held in my front lap. I whispered to my teacher that I needed the hall pass to return to the nurse's office because of my period stain. Without any hesitation, she reached into a drawer of her desk, handed me her hall pass, and immediately returned to her lesson plan, not giving me a second thought. I turned my heel and made another frustrating trip back down to the nurse's office, quietly cursing the whole process under my breath.

The nurse handed me a thick, generic pad to change in her private restroom and then advised me to call my mother so she could bring me a new pair of pants. To my surprise, Mom actually answered the phone. I explained what happened and that I needed new pants. About thirty minutes later, she showed up, handed me a grocery bag, and quickly left. She didn't even wait for me to hand her the dirty jeans back or ask if I was okay.

When I returned to the restroom to change, inside the bag, I found a wrinkled pair of worn jeans that she had pulled from the hamper. "Did I not have any clean jeans?!" I angrily thought. She also didn't think to include a fresh pair of underwear.

I discovered my inner thighs were even stained a light pink from the blood, and I soaked paper towels to wipe them clean. After dressing, I examined myself in the mirror and hated what I saw.

The jeans Mom packed me were disheveled, and they didn't complement the style of shirt or shoes I had worn. The chunky black mules stood out like clown shoes because the cuffs of the jeans were the wrong cut and style, and the shirt was now too oversize. It looked as though I had no fashion sense. And I didn't! The outfit I dressed in that morning was one of my first thoughtful and intentional looks. I wanted to look fashionable, but now, it was the complete opposite for the rest of the school day. I wished my mom had just checked me out of school for the day. It was the cutoff jeans shorts moment all over again.

Not So Thankful

It was the Thanksgiving break of my eighth-grade year. Schools tend to give students a week off so they can have enough time to travel and spend time with family. Since Mom didn't have any family in the US, we had no one to travel to for a visit. Instead, I was enjoying sleeping in late each morning and staying up late at night.

On Thursday afternoon, the phone rang. Mom answered it and a moment later, hands me the phone. "It's your dad," she told me.

"Hi, Pa! Happy Thanksgiving!" I answered excitedly.

I hadn't seen or heard from my dad in a while, and I wasn't expecting to get a call from him. The last time I had seen him, it was quite the ordeal.

Pa stopped by our apartment and knocked on our door. He was an addict at this time and most likely homeless again. Pa had a distinct way of knocking, a melodic pattern, so we knew it was him without having to look through the peephole or ask aloud who it was.

Maybe it was pre-teen angst or because it had been a while since I had seen or heard from him and therefore felt resentment, but for whatever reason, I told Mom I wasn't in the mood to speak with him. That was a first for me.

Behind the closed door, Mom told him I wasn't home.

"Where is she?!" Pa asked irritably.

"I don't know, but she's not here!" Mom boldly replied.

"What do you mean you don't know?! Where is she?! I want to speak to my daughter!" Pa demanded in anger as he punched the door between each question.

Suddenly, glass shattered.

I sprinted to the living room to show Pa I was home in hopes that it would calm him down, but I was too late. He had punched through the living room window. Mom swiftly reached up to snatch the iron horseshoe that hung by a red string above the doorway for luck. She then flung open the door, took aim, and hurled the iron shoe at my dad. Mom wasn't afraid to fight back, even after all he had put her through.

The horseshoe hit him square in the back. He flinched from the contact as he quickly pedaled away on a bike. A neighbor, who heard the commotion, came out of their apartment and witnessed my dad getting hit by the horseshoe. The neighbor picked up the horseshoe, brought it over to my mom, asked her if we were okay, and then commended my mom on her aim.

I felt guilty for avoiding my dad and causing a fracas. But based on his behavior and reaction, he was most likely drunk or high.

One weekend during a sleepover with my cousins, my aunt invited me to join the family to visit her brother at the cemetery. Michael, their younger brother, died in 1984, one year before I was born.

We drove far north to the cemetery. When we arrived, we kids gathered on a bench, under a large oak tree nearest to Tío Michael's headstone. I sat and watched my Tía Sonia dust the headstone and place flowers in the brass vase which was tethered to the headstone by a chain. She then shared the story about how he died.

I've heard two accounts of what happened leading to Michael's death. The first version suggests Pa and Tío Miguel were driving to another city, at night, when Pa lost control of the vehicle and slammed into a semi truck. The accident killed my uncle, who had been asleep in the passenger seat before the crash. He died in the fiery wreck.

The other version suggests my dad declined to join his brother to drive to another city. Michael, en route to his destination, was involved in a major vehicle accident that resulted in a car fire and killed him.

My Tía Sonia recalled hearing about the accident on the local news but had no idea it involved her own brother. My father and his sister, Gloria, then drove to the small town to claim his body. Finally, at the coroner's office, the only identifiable part of Michael was his left forearm featuring a nude figure of a woman tattoo.

Some suggest it was the survivor's guilt that led my dad to seek out hard drugs to self-medicate from the pain. I feel it was a combination of many traumas.

Regardless of any person's traumatic upbringing, it does not give them permission to be abusive toward others.

"Hi, mija. I'm in the hospital," Pa told me, in a melancholy tone.

"Oh no, what's wrong? What happened?" I asked him.

"The doctors tell me that I have cancer."

He then went on to describe the day he landed in the hospital. Because it was the holiday season, he was attempting to get sober and work again. This was my dad's habitual cycle of constantly getting on and off the sober wagon.

That morning, he got dressed for work, but before making his way to the shop, he stopped at Sunny's convenience store. While inside the store, he fainted and was found passed out on the floor. The Sunny's clerk called 911, and an ambulance took my father to Memorial Hermann Southwest Hospital.

The owners and employees of this Sunny's knew my dad and his side of the family well - as it's on the same block as the apartment complex they all lived in, and they frequently shopped there - so they were easily able to track someone down and inform them of my dad's whereabouts.

My dad went on to tell me that the doctors would run more tests and strongly suggested quickly scheduling surgery. I could tell from his tone and energy that this was serious.

"When do you get out?" I asked with concern.

"I don't know, mija," he said, sounding discouraged.

That night, I kept asking Mom questions, "Where is Pa going to live?" "Is he going to get better?" "Can we go visit him at the hospital?" "When can I see him?" and so on, but she had no answers to give me.

Mom allowed Pa to move in with us, again, since he was sick and would need a place to recover post-surgery. But the apartment lease would be expiring soon, and Mom had no plans to renew.

Pa moved in, and I was happy to have him sober and in my life again. He was happy being with us, too. He enjoyed cooking, so one afternoon, Mom and I went to the grocery store to pick up the ingredients he needed for dinner. We returned home and began unpacking the purchases. Pa stood in front of the sink and began washing the produce.

"Where are the limes? I asked for limes," he said in a gruff tone.

In that same moment, I had just pulled the produce bag of limes out of the grocery bag, and in my preteen angst, I flung the bag of limes towards his face so he could see them, and responded with, "Here they are!"

Although my fist holding the produce bag stopped before hitting his face, the inertia of the swift movement kept the weight of the limes swinging, and they hit the right side of his cheek. Time froze. In that instant, fear coursed through my body. I was anticipating his elbow or fist to knock my teeth out or knock me out of consciousness completely. I knew I had made a mistake and regretted it instantaneously. Mom stood on the other side of Pa, and though I was frozen, I shifted my eyes away from him to look at her, and the concern on her face had me even more convinced that I was about to feel his wrath. Her face read as though she knew he would hit me for the disrespect, but probably take it too far like he did with her, and she would have to physically fight him off to defend me. All of these thoughts ran through my mind in a millisecond.

Pa's right hand flew up and snatched me by my left wrist, which had still been held up beside his face, and pulled my arm down so fast that I bent down towards its direction and let out a light yelp from the shock.

"Don'tchu EVER again disrespect me like that!" he bellowed.

Pa yanked the bag of limes from my hand and returned to washing the produce. I know it must have taken every grain of patience in him not to have hit me. In contrast to his relationship with my mom, Pa never disciplined me. Not even a spanking.

Mom discreetly gestured for me to follow her out of the kitchen to give him space. We quietly walked away to our own corners of the house to forget what happened. It was a delicious but quiet dinner that night.

Pa began to distance himself. He wasn't as chatty with me or Mom. He had spoken with the leasing office and signed a new lease for the same apartment we were living in since Mom wasn't renewing hers. With this, he assumed Mom and I would soon be moving out.

I spoke with Mom and explained that I wanted to stay living with my dad. She shrugged her shoulders with a flat, "Okay," and went about her day.

When Pa got back from work that evening and began removing his boots, I sat beside him and said, "Pa, I want to stay here with you."

His mood instantly lifted as he sat up, looked me in the eye with a great big smile, and hugged me. "Thank you, mija. This makes me so happy."

Immediately after Mom moved out, Pa began refurnishing the apartment. He brought in a sofa set and a dining table set that he purchased from his extended family. These were all pre-owned but they looked and felt new to me. He bought a twin-sized bed for himself and new bedding. He slowly began purchasing things such as lamps, cooking and dish sets, and more.

Pa let me keep one of Mom's cats, Chiquita. He liked Chiquita because she would knead biscuits on his back, making it feel like a back massage. We also had a red betta fish, and I even got a hamster. It felt more like a home than ever before.

Eventually, it was time for Pa's scheduled surgery. We were hopeful they would be able to cut out the cancer located in his colon. We all waited in the waiting room of the hospital. When Pa was wheeled back into his recovery room, the doctor asked to speak with us out in the hall so that Pa could rest.

Erica, along with my aunts, cousins, and I, all stood around the doctor waiting for the prognosis.

"As soon as we opened him up, we found that the cancer had metastasized all over his lower abdomen. There was nothing we could do, so we closed him back up," the doctor said apathetically.

My cousin was quickly trying to translate for my aunts, then my Tía Estella began to sob.

"What now?" we asked.

"Well, we will set him up with chemotherapy in hopes it will shrink the rather large tumors and reassess at a later time," the doctor responded. Then he excused himself.

We stood around in shock and in tears, not understanding what this meant for my dad. Or how much time we had left with him.

After Pa's diagnosis, we planned a family beach day. Mom even agreed to come along, and Erica brought my toddler-niece, Mona.

Upon arrival, we set up camp. Towels on the sand, snacks and beverages out, and so on. We lathered Mona in sunblock even though the weather was windy and overcast. Better to be safe than sorry. Plus, she was so pale she could burn on a cloudy day.

Mona wore the cutest little pink two-piece swimsuit with ruffles on the hips. She posed for the camera, "Click!"

It was too cold to swim, so Mona and I stuck to wading ankle deep and building sand castles. During this time, Erica, Mom, and Pa began unpacking the rest of the food. The seagulls knew what time it was and began to swarm! There seemed to be hundreds of them, and all were squawking loudly!

Since we're all animal lovers, we felt they needed to be fed. We began tossing chips, pretzels, crackers, and other dry goods onto the sand. Soon, we noticed some birds were coming in closer and catching the snacks midair! It gave Pa an idea.

Pa asked Erica, Mona, and me to get ready for a picture, pointing out where he wanted us to stand, and then he handed Mom the disposable camera. He then squatted down, scooped up a fistful of pretzels in his hand, split them evenly between both hands and hurried over to the girls and me. He tossed the snacks up high and over behind us while yelling, "Take the picture!"

In this picture, Pa and Mona are posed, camera-ready, while Erica and I are seen laughing, all with a curtain of seagulls behind us. It was a perfect family day at the beach.

Religion vs Spirituality

During Pa's sober stints, he would devote his faith back to Christianity. When he was back on the sober wagon, he would clean up his life by securing a place to stay, working, and joining a church.

It wasn't always the same church. Different buildings, different people, but always the same God.

On the weekends that I slept over when I was little, Pa would wake me early Sunday mornings. No sleeping in on the day of rest, funny enough. Pa would dress me, give me a shot of Dimetapp medicine, and we'd stop for breakfast at McDonald's before finally arriving at the congregation.

Upon arrival, we'd have the obligatory hellos as we slowly made our way to the classrooms. The children were entertained in the classrooms and taught basic biblical stories while the adults were in the big church for praise and worship before kicking off the sermon.

The children's classes did not last as long and ended before the sermons. Therefore, we would be led in a single file line to the main church and scattered to find our parents. Once I found Pa, I would shuffle down to the pew to sit beside him. This was the boring part. Having to sit silently still while a man with a monotone voice spoke in a language I wasn't fluent in. If it wasn't the sermon that put me to sleep, it was the grape-flavored Dimetapp.

My mother, on the other hand, was spiritual. She believes in tarot, astrology, fairies, and other-worldly beliefs. Because of her unconventional views and my father's opposing dogmatic stance, I was told that what my mother believed was evil. The Bible teaches that those who follow the occult are followers of Satan, the devil. Satan was cast out of Heaven and is known as God's enemy. Therefore, anyone who is a follower of God's enemy is also God's enemy and ours by extension.

There was even a cruel rumor that my mother cast witchcraft on my father, hexing him with cancer. The funny thing about that accusation is, I believe it was God who gave my father cancer. Not as karma or to atone for his many sins, but to give my father back to me. Even for a short, difficult time.

My greatest fear as a child was that my father would die of an overdose or, worse, be murdered. His body left out on the street, rotting in a ditch or alleyway. When he may eventually be found, the coroner would be unable to identify him. We'd never know he had passed. He would have been buried in an unmarked grave, leaving behind a family that would never heal.

During Pa's battle with cancer, we were members of the Restoration Outreach church. This organization specializes in helping men get sober. The Pastor had a second home on his property that housed these men. The men in this group were then dubbed "The Homeboys." It was treated much like a rehab center.

To join, the men would have to accept staying and having no contact with family or friends for at least three months. In addition, they would be required to attend services, bible studies, and other group outings. The men would be given a Bible, clothes, a bed, and chores. Each man would pitch in to support with cooking, cleaning, and so forth. Many men together in one small house can soon become very dirty. But this home would discipline those who did not follow suit. Nothing abusive, just more chores. My dad was a "Homeboy" and was living at this home when Erica gave birth to my niece. At this point, he was considered a leader in the home, and with a buddy, aka chaperon, he could visit Erica in the hospital to meet his granddaughter, Angela-Antonia. A combination of my mom's and his namesakes.

I, too, became a follower of this church. I even called the Pastor's daughters my best friends. And Gina, my childhood best friend, became a "Jesus Freak," a moniker young Christians refer to themselves as after the popular contemporary Christian-themed song by DC Talk. But Gina and her family attended a different church.

When we all got together for sleepovers at my and Pa's place, my friends and I would hang out in the bedroom and pray. On a prayer night sleepover, Gina told us that the Holy Spirit was unsettling her. She felt heaviness and darkness in the room. I had no idea what evil we had invited into our home and why it was there. We all searched around the room as if we were going to find a voodoo doll or a goat's head under my bed. Gina then pointed at a frame on the wall.

The artwork in the thin, black plastic frame was one of Nagel's "ladies of the 80s" posters. I was confused. This was simply a drawing of some 1980s model my mom admired. It wasn't a demon, a vampire, or a cursed object. But then I thought, maybe it was evil just by association. Because my mom followed Satan's practices, that meant that everything she owned was inherently evil, right?

"It was my mom's! She left it here when she moved out," I announced.

"It's evil. We need to pray over it, anoint it with oil, throw it away in the garbage outside, and then we'll cleanse the room." Gina determined.

So we did just that, taking down everything mom left behind, and into the garbage it went. She even had me take down Disney-branded items like a Winnie the Pooh picture frame. Apparently, Disney was a tool of the Devil, too.

When Mom came to look for her personal belongings sometime later, we informed her that we had thrown them away. She was extremely upset. She began questioning why we would do such a thing. Embarrassment, regret, and shame made me feel I shouldn't dare look her in the face. Our actions basically showed my mom that we didn't respect her, that she was evil and followed evil, and that we judged her for her interests.

What gave us the right or the entitlement? My mother is a woman who loves animals and tries to save them. Cats, dogs, birds, possums, and so on. You name it, we probably had it. This she does in homage to the Virgin Mary. A woman who vows to help innocent and forgotten animals should not be considered evil.

Being "saved" can become dangerous to those who do not proclaim to be followers of Christ. Heck, even if you are a Christian but part of a different denomination, that can be an issue. I began judging people so harshly and literally feared for their eternal souls. I spent hours praying for my family and friends to save their souls, but that was also accompanied by treating them like ignorant fools.

During my freshman year in high school, I joined the Christian Club after-school program. When I walked in, a girl named Eva waved me over. Eva had beautiful tan-golden skin, green hazel eyes, bright white teeth, and a mole near her lip like Supermodel Cindy Crawford. She always wore long skirts. Even jean skirts. I learned it was because she was Pentecostal, and it was required for women to dress modestly, which meant no short or tight-fitting skirts, and never pants. Eva began to introduce me to other students in the group, and when she introduced me to a boy I recognized from my English class, I said,

"I didn't know you were a Christian! You don't act like it in class."

He looked down, ashamed. A few kids snickered. I hadn't meant it in a cruel way, but sometimes that's how immature Christians behave towards others.

Shortly after joining the group, my dad began to feel very ill and asked Eva's mom in the parking lot if I could stay with them the night so he could go to the hospital.

Pa must have been desperate because he did not know these people from Adam. He had just introduced himself and knew they were Christian. After they exchanged phone numbers, I kissed Pa goodbye and hopped into their minivan.

We drove to the city of Rosenberg, where their Pentecostal church was located. At the end of the sermon, their Pastor asked the near-empty church if anyone wanted to commit to Jesus.

The Pastor made eye contact with me, pointed directly at me, and into the mic said in Spanish:

"You there, daughter, do you want to be saved tonight?"

I furrowed my brows in confusion and annoyance. Could he not sense my Holy Spirit?!

Eva quickly leaned forward, waving her arms and shaking her head in a "no" manner, interceding on my behalf in Spanish.

"She's already saved!" Eva said.

He just shook his head in agreement, not apologizing. In my head, I tried to read his thoughts. "He's judging me for wearing jean pants, or simply because he's never met me before, and therefore I must not know Jesus. He probably assumes Eva introduced me to Christ, saving my damned soul and earning herself an upgrade in Heaven." I left their church upset. Her family attempted to apologize while avoiding speaking ill of their leader.

I never stayed at their home or visited their church again. My church wasn't that judgmental. Or so I thought.

Looking back, there were instances in which my own congregation treated others unfairly. We judged girls for wearing jeans that were considered "too tight" when really, they were just well-fitted pants on a curvy young lady. The ushers didn't permit these young ladies to dance during praise and worship. We judged couples, and even ousted members, for having premarital sex. We judged people who didn't live by the standards we set for ourselves. We were hypocrites. We weren't following Jesus' teaching, to simply love one another.

Driver's Ed.

During the spring semester of my freshman year at Lee High School, a driving school visited our campus. The driving program set up an info booth in the cafeteria, handing out pamphlets to entice students to enroll in their next course.

I walked over to their table and eagerly picked up a pamphlet to take home.

That night, while Pa was preparing dinner, I told him about the opportunity to learn to drive at school and that I was interested. When we sat to eat, he reviewed the pamphlet I left for him to read. Pa skimmed over the pages of the trifold and said he would think about it.

That weekend at church, I overheard Pa speaking to the other members about it. And then later that afternoon, when we were at Tía Estella's apartment visiting for lunch, they discussed it too. To my delight, it seemed everyone was encouraging him to enroll me.

Although I was only fourteen, the timeline would work in my favor. I technically could begin the classroom phase of the education course at my age. The minimum age requirement to apply for a license was fifteen, and I was only a few weeks shy of qualifying for a Hardship License.

In Texas, A Texas Hardship License can be granted to someone as young as fifteen. Because Pa was battling cancer, he was technically medically disabled, and since it was just the two of us, if there were ever an emergency, I may have had to be the designated person to take him to a hospital. I didn't want to wait another year until I was sixteen. I didn't know if we had that much time.

Pa surprised me with a money order to enroll in the course. I practically skipped to the cafeteria, waving it in the air above me. When they asked for my age, I mentioned I would be fifteen by the time the in-class portion ended and sitting behind the wheel began. They didn't bat an eye, and I was officially enrolled in driver's ed.

The course was held after school in a classroom I'd never been in, filled with students I had never met. I didn't have any friends sign up with me, so I took a seat in the last row. You know, where the cool kids sit.

We each received a yellow driver's education booklet and began learning the basics of the Texas Department of Safety & Laws.

Our class was split up into groups for the driving portion. Unfortunately, the first crew was involved in a major accident! One boy had a broken leg fitted with a cast an all, while the instructor had a broken wrist and arm in a sling. That caused some nerves for me.

After what felt like an entire semester, the day finally arrived to move the classroom from behind a desk to behind the wheel. We met in the parking lot across the street from the high school. The instructor took attendance and called one of the students to sit in the driver's seat while she sat in the front passenger seat. The remaining three of us squeezed into the backseat.

I paid close attention to everything the instructor said to the student driver, but when she called my name, I gulped.

I opened the rear passenger door to slide out and make my way around to the driver's seat. I followed the "D, Triple S, M" motto they taught us. This stands for "Doors, Seat belt, Steering Wheel, Seat, and Mirrors." All the things you must adequately adjust to prepare for safe driving.

Then, I turned the key to switch on the ignition, and I looked over at the instructor sitting next to me, waiting for instructions.

"Drive," she said bluntly.

"I've never driven before," I confessed.

"Well, what do you think you're here for?" she responded in irritation.

She must've been in her fifties to sixties, sporting a short buzz cut style hair, deep wrinkles, and a smoker's voice.

"Put it in drive, and let's go!" she demanded.

I pushed my right foot into the brake pedal and switched gears from "Park" to the big "D," drive. Three clicks.

I slowly released the pressure off the brake, and the car began rolling forward. She instructed me to give it some gas and make a left at the end of the parking row. I made about two or three loops around the parking lot before it was time to switch with another student to have their turn. Turns out, it wasn't that hard!

We drove around the Richmond, Westheimer, and Galleria neighborhoods for more learning and experience. Funny, Richmond Avenue was the same street young people would cruise around in on Saturday nights causing traffic for no reason, hopping out of cars to get phone numbers and meet up.

I passed my course before my last driving lesson. My instructor gave me the form needed for the DMV. That's how well I picked up driving. My instructor trusted me. Too bad for the only girl who failed. Her parents bought her a new Mitsubishi Eclipse and everything. She really was a bad driver, and the instructor said it wasn't safe for her to be on the road yet. I agreed.

I didn't have a car. I mean, we had a car, or I really mean, Pa had a small pickup truck with a standard engine. The kind that typical Salvadoran men prefer to drive. I think it reminds them of their youth. The new tires he put on after buying the truck from another Salvadoran had blue wall paint. They looked a lot like the Salvadoran flag after they were installed.

Because it was an older model, Pa installed an aftermarket stereo, the kind with the removable face, so no one would break in and steal it. We used it to play our CDs, although Pa still used the old cassette player in the truck, as that's what was mostly available at the church store: worship music on cassette tapes. It probably goes without saying, but we only played Christian music or sermons in this ride. But that wasn't a big deal for me; I enjoyed the music and sermons.

To most people, learning to drive a standard is a little more intimidating than driving an automatic. Shifting gears means you can't always have your hands on "10" and "2", then using both feet to maintain the clutch, gas, and brakes seems like a lot.

I passed the class and made my way to the Department of Motor Vehicles to officially apply for my Driver's Permit. I passed the written exam on the first attempt, and thanks to the course I completed, I didn't need another driving test. I was so ecstatic when I had my permit in hand. Although it looked much like a voter's registration card, I flashed it to anyone who would give me the time of day. At church with all my friends, I would brag about the instructor handing me my certificate of completion before the final test.

One Sunday, after morning service, my best friends and I got the idea that it would be fun for me to drive us to the Galleria Mall. I would just have to borrow someone's car (a car with an automatic engine, of course). I would also need a chaperon because it was still a Learner's Permit I was using, so an adult with a valid driver's license needed to join.

We chose Sister Maria; this way it was a "Girl's Trip." Pa was going home for lunch to do our laundry and rest.

Brother Mike was a youth leader who drove a blue Toyota Rav4. I walked straight up to Mike and asked, "May I please borrow your car to drive Angie, Vero, Maria and me to the Galleria? PLEASE!"

He quickly snapped, "No!"

I refused to take no for an answer. I had my permit and was formally educated in the aspect of driving, so I could totally be trusted. I wanted to show off my driving skills and celebrate with my friends at the mall.

Looking back, I now understand why Mike didn't want to let me, a fifteen-year-old girl with practically zero driving experience and no insurance, drive his car on Houston freeways and into one of the most congested areas with frequent accidents.

But, I digress; after lots and lots of begging and pleading while chasing him around the church campus, he finally relented and handed me his keys. I screamed and jumped over to the girls to share in my excitement. We ran over to his car, giddy. Sister Maria sat in the front passenger seat while Angie, Vero, and little Tina buckled up in the back seat.

"D, Triple S, and M," I said to myself, going through the motions, hoping the others would notice how responsible I was. Then, we were off! The girls in the back waved to churchgoers, and we drove away.

It had rained earlier that morning and small pools of water in the street reflected the day like obsidian mirrors. I continued down Cavalcade until I crossed underneath 610. I dropped my left hand„ allowing my weight to switch down the left turn signal. When the light turned green, I let out a deep exhale to calm my nerves.

I placed my hands firmly at 10 and 2, and pressed my right foot into the gas pedal to increase speed. I could feel the tires meet the road through these contact points.

I made it onto 610, and I had less than half a mile to switch lanes before I was forced to take the fork leading me to I-45 North. I switched my left signal back on and checked my rear view and left mirror before looking over my left shoulder out the window to ensure all was clear to switch lanes.

It all happened so fast. One second, the lane was clear; a half second later, I look to my left again, and another car was slowly merging into the same lane I was in.

I immediately freaked out, and to avoid crashing, I gripped the steering wheel and yanked it to the right to swing back into our original lane. I over corrected and lost control of the vehicle. We began to hydroplane, and the car spun clockwise uncontrollably. Everyone was screaming, and my eyes were shut tight. I slammed on the brake, and as quickly as it started, it ended. The car came to a complete standstill, and everyone was silent. My chest rose and dropped rapidly. I opened my eyes to look around. Maria had her hands gripped to the door and dash. Looking past her outside the passenger window, I saw all the cars on the freeway had stopped and were slowly beginning to drive away. Miraculously, the car stopped in the far-left emergency lane. This meant we spun across five lanes of highway traffic and stopped before slamming into the concrete barrier.

"Okay, let's just switch seats and I will drive us back to the church," Maria said, breaking the silence.

I nodded in agreement and unbuckled my seat belt. I quickly stepped out of the vehicle and ran around the back of the car to the front passenger seat.

After I buckled my seat belt, the weight of what just happened and what could have happened washed over me. I put four other people at risk, and I was both embarrassed and filled with shame. What was supposed to be a dream moment of me showing off and celebrating, turned into a nightmare.

Maria made the short distance drive back to church, but it might as well have been across the country. It felt like the longest drive of my life.

When we walked into the church, those who were still there already knew what had happened. Turned out, the pastor's wife, Angie and Vero's mom, was driving not far behind us and witnessed the entire thing. She picked up her cell phone and called Pastor Joe in panic. She was driving at a high speed and could not stop on the freeway. She reported seeing us spinning across several lanes on the freeway and in front of semi trucks, no less. She was worried we would be hit and begged him to send someone from the church to drive over and check on us.

I was mortified that everyone knew what I had done and terrified of what my dad's reaction would be. What would he say? What would he do? I would have to wait in dread until he returned to church for evening service to find out.

As evening service approached, I asked my friends to let me sit in the middle of the pew between them. I did this so that when my dad showed up, I was somewhat hidden.

Those of us who show up to church early, about fifteen minutes before service begins, turn towards our seats to kneel and pray. During prayer, every time I closed my eyes, it felt as though I was back in the driver's seat of the car, spinning out of control. You know that feeling you get when you're out on a boat for a day, and when you return to land, your body can still feel waves rocking you back and forth from the inside? Needless to say, I was unable to focus on praying, and so instead I kept my eyes open and worried about what my dad would say.

At the end of the service and the final "amen," I said goodbye to my friends as they walked me to my dad's car.

Pa didn't speak a word to me the whole ride home. My anxiety and nerves spiked! I was imagining all the different ways my dad's anger would manifest itself. Would he yell at me? Ground me? Hit me? My anxiety was running wild.

We pull into our apartment complex. It was dark out with only soft amber lights flowing from a couple of posts in the parking lot. Pa parked and turned off the engine. I was paralyzed with fear, not knowing what was next, and then he got out of the truck. The door shut behind him, and so I exited the truck too. I walked slowly, staying several paces behind him, toward the apartment, potentially my doom, and I watched him unlock the door and step inside. Deep exhale. There was no avoiding it now.

Pa stood holding the front door open for me. I kept my eyes down and stepped over the threshold, walked past him, and took a few steps inside.

I stopped in the middle of the living room with my back still facing him.

Apologize. I'm just going to apologize and beg for forgiveness. I

147

should not have asked Brother Mike for his car. I should not have asked Sister Maria to be my chaperone. I should not have had Angie, Vero, and Tina in the car. I should have known the conditions for driving on wet roads were unsafe. I should have known better, and I was sorry.

"Pa, I'm sor-" I did not finish my sentence.

Pa had thrown his arms around me and squeezed me into a tight embrace.

For a split second, I was shocked and confused. Why was Pa hugging me and not chastising me? Then it hit me.

Pa was grateful I was not hurt. Happy that I was home and still with him. That broke my heart. Tears welled up behind my eyelids, and my nerves and anxiety disappeared but were quickly replaced by more shame and guilt. The lump in my throat grew into a hard rock, and the stinging in my nose forced me to scrunch up my face to try and make it go away.

My dad was actively dying, and I can only imagine what was running through his mind. Here he was, fearing not only for his life but for mine too. And there I was, putting myself and others in danger. How would a father ever recover? The rest of his life would be so dark. He would undoubtedly stop fighting and allow the cancer to take over.

I'm grateful for the miracle that managed to keep us safe. Spinning across several lanes of high-speed traffic, with several cars and semi trucks, on a slick road was nothing short of a miracle. God and the angels were indeed watching over us.

A Scholarship

An essay contest was announced at school. Pa was undergoing chemotherapy cancer treatment while also working full-time. Although my dad was a legal Resident, he had to be paid under the table, in cash, in order for us to continue receiving government benefits. These benefits included his disability checks, food stamps, and health insurance. The legal system defines this as a crime, but the actual crime, I feel, is people living below the poverty level. What he did was for our survival. Pa was a single dad battling late-stage colon cancer. He worked full-time through every chemo round, commuting long distances six days a week to work no matter how badly he suffered from the side effects. I can think of a few other things that feel more criminal than a father fighting for his life and to provide for his young daughter. My father, when sober, was a provider and a soldier.

The money my dad received for his disability was five hundred dollars a month. We lived in a one-bedroom apartment in a low-income neighborhood. Our rent alone was more than that amount, not including other bills: utilities, a phone bill, his truck loan, and all other basic necessities. Food stamps helped, but he had to work to make ends meet. As a teenager, I was naive and didn't understand or comprehend the concept of money and bills. Although we weren't rich and couldn't afford to travel for leisure, our basic needs were met. We credited God for giving Pa the strength to work and helped bless us to make ends meet.

After reading the guidelines for the scholarship contest, I decided to write about Harriett Tubman. I learned about this historical figure and the Underground Railroad in the fifth grade during Black History Month. The story of heroism stayed with me because of the similarities to our largely immigrant community. When the adults would listen to the news or speak about people "crossing," it would remind me of the stories of slaves escaping the South and traveling North via the Underground Railroad. Immigrants crossing the U.S. border illegally then, and sadly even now, would be chased by law officers, if not by horse, then by car, or even by air. They still use dogs, too. More similarities. To the teenage me, it felt current and somewhat relatable.

"Intro, body, body, body, and conclusion," I said to myself as I began to draft the frame of my essay, using the writing method I learned in elementary school when preparing for the "TAAS" test, the standardized Texas Assessment of Academic Skills.

I worked on my writing process chart to outline my main idea and ideas to support that until I had enough content to begin my first draft. I handwrote my essay using the provided sheets for official submission. When I was done, I walked into the main office and added it to the tray of entries. That had been my first visit to the office; it felt so foreign to me, even though it was located in the high school.

Weeks later, the school held a mandatory assembly, so we children were herded like cattle into the auditorium. The school head principal, an older white man, welcomed the students and gave an introduction to present a guest speaker. He handed the microphone to a tall, Black man who appeared to be young, maybe in his twenties or thirties based on his trendy threads and sneakers. The audience quieted down, signaling respect to a man who looked more like them. The speaker introduced himself by name and the organization he was affiliated with; it was the same organization that hosted the essay contest.

"Oh, I submitted an entry for that contest a while back," I thought to myself. I had forgotten about it altogether.

After speaking for a couple more minutes, explaining his role in the organization and its mission, he said they were ready to announce the contest winners. He then added that each winner would receive ten thousand dollars towards their college fund. My ears perked right up!

"Did he really say *ten thousand dollars?!*" I asked myself.

I didn't remember that being mentioned during the initial contest announcement. I figured it would be a thousand dollars, max.

The speaker pulled an index card from his coat pocket and held it up. "Winners, please meet me at the front after the assembly. Without further ado, the winners are..."

My name was called.

Pa was ecstatic when I told him, smiling a big, cheesy grin and giving God thanks. At church that Sunday, it was my father's turn to speak on the importance of tithes and offerings. People who are active members of a congregation are expected to participate in giving 10 percent of their earned wages to the church. This helps fund the building to pay for utilities, maintenance, the pastor's salary, and more. Offerings are separate; additional donations are made above the tithe. This is the infamous bowl that gets passed around a few times during services. Back in biblical days, people gave ten percent of their crop yield or prized livestock to sacrifice as offerings. The church also preaches that God will bless you tenfold for paying your tithes and giving monetary offerings. I would even pay 10 percent of my allowance. If Pa gave me a twenty-dollar bill, I would present at least two dollars to the church.

"Tonight, I have a testimony to share," Pa announced from behind the pulpit.

"God has blessed me for faithfully paying my tithes; even when I think I can't possibly spare it, I trust in Him because God is great. This week, my daughter received an incredible and unexpected blessing. Betty received a ten-thousand-dollar college scholarship!"

The congregation went wild.

"GOD IS GOOD!" he proclaimed.

I "raised the roof" with my arms while smiling ear to ear to express how proud and excited I was that God had blessed us. Everyone looked so happy for us. My dad was beaming on that stage, and he looked straight at me. Pa was filled with pride and maybe a sense of security for my educational future. I, too, shared those sentiments. I was proud for many reasons. For having submitted the essay, for making my dad proud, for being a living testimony that paying tithes would bring blessings, and for securing myself a way to support college tuition. My faith led me to believe we were being taken care of by a higher spirit and that everything was falling into place.

When I came home from school and walked through the door, I noticed that my dad was home. It was unusual, as he usually wouldn't arrive home after work until close to dinner. Pa had a surprise waiting for me.

He led me to the dining room, where I found a new gym bag on the table. The bag was open and filled with all sorts of things. Candy bars, roasted and salted sunflower seeds, a journal, several new colorful gel pens, a flashlight, and more!

Pa explained that the school had called him for a meeting, so he went to the school's main office. He was given specific instructions on what to buy and do to prepare me for a trip. He then explained what clothes and toiletry supplies I would need to pack because I was going on a retreat.

The scholarship organization was hosting a retreat for all the winning students. Soon, the day arrived for us students to meet and depart for our trip. That morning, Pa woke me early and prepared a toasted plain bagel filled with lots of cream cheese and fresh avocado. I could taste the love. He carried my bag to the truck, and off we went. We drove onto Chimney Rock Road; then he took the on-ramp to 610 North. We exited shortly after and pulled into a hotel parking lot in the Galleria area. Leaving the stereo on, Pa parked the truck, and Marcos Witt, a Spanish worship singer, played in the background. We didn't speak. We were both nervous. I still hadn't determined where or who I was going with. He didn't know who he was entrusting me to.

Four high schools participated in the contest, each with a handful of student winners. When the coach bus pulled in, we noticed other kids my age getting out of cars, all carrying bags, so my dad signaled for us to follow suit. I stayed close to my dad's side, holding his hand as we walked to the bus door. I covertly looked at the others but didn't recognize any students.

Two younger-looking adults with clipboards and lanyards call for everyone's attention. They introduced themselves and thanked the parents for getting the students to the rendezvous point on time. It was time to depart. Pa and I turned to each other for a hug and kiss

153

goodbye. He instructed me to be good and to say my prayers; I shook my head in acknowledgment. I said goodbye and made my way onto the bus.

On the first night of our retreat, after dinner, our leader, the same man who announced my name as a winner that fateful day I recognized, instructed us to open our letters. He read our perplexed faces as we students were unaware of any letters. The leader informed us that our parents or guardians wrote us letters, which we would find in the back of our journals.

I grabbed my new journal from my bag, flipped to the back, and found an envelope. Inside was a handwritten note from my father. It was so heartfelt and moved me to tears. In the letter, Pa expressed how proud he was of me and grateful to God for giving him the gift of such an amazing daughter.

The retreat was intended to nurture the students who showed academic promise and drive. The goal was to connect us with mentors and leaders who would help ensure our success in graduating from high school and using our scholarships. During our time together, we participated in several activities to build our self-esteem and self-confidence, and make new connections and friends so that those of us in the same schools had each other to rely on once we returned.

The first activity we performed in a group setting consisted of students queuing up in a line to approach the group leader holding a wooden board. The leader then explained that the board represented limiting beliefs and that we each needed to find the strength to overcome such obstacles. So, one by one, each student walked up towards the board, and with one swift chop of the arm, they cracked the board in half, similar to what you see in karate-themed movies. Finally, it was my turn. I approached my board, took a deep breath, raised my hand, and swiftly swung it down to meet the wood.

"Thump!"

Silence and embarrassment. I did not crack the wood. The first kid to fail.

The leader said, "It's okay, try again! You've got this."

I snapped it on the second attempt.

In another activity, we were instructed to read a sentence silently to ourselves: "Opportunity is NOWHERE." When the leader asked us what we read, nearly in unison, the group responded, "Opportunity is NOW HERE!"

Well, I said, "Opportunity is NO WHERE."

I wonder what that had to say about my psyche.

What I found interesting was that I could easily spot our similarities, not in terms of race or gender, but in economic status. You could see it in our hairstyles, clothes, shoes, lack of trending accessories, and so on. We were the poor kids from the poor school districts. But we were also the bright and promising minds of our peers. Our essays revealed we had what it takes to get us ahead and one day out of poverty. That made me proud of our little motley crew.

Mi Quince

I was a dama in my prima's quinceañera, meaning I was part of the birthday girl's court. A Latina's quince is a major milestone in her transition from a girl to becoming a woman. Although it is a cultural, Catholic religious rite, by the 90s, it felt more like being about the party. A big party. Like a wedding sans groom.

You have a full court of damas and chambelanes, you have a limo, a professional photographer, a church site, a reception site, catering, a DJ, decor, and more.

After the church ceremony, and once we were at the reception site, there was a formal introduction of Brenda becoming a woman. Part of this introduction included us, her court, performing a waltz to Chayanne's "Tiempo de Valz." We even had a baile de sorpresa, which is the surprise dance we choreographed, to the Back Street Boys' hit song "Everybody." It really was a beautiful ceremony and a memorable party.

When my fifteenth birthday began approaching, Pa asked if I wanted my own quinceañera. Considering this proposal, I began to think of the big party we could throw. But then I wrestled with the fact that I wouldn't be able to play any secular music, and therefore, my friends outside of church wouldn't enjoy it. Who would we invite? I only had a few aunts, uncles, and cousins on my dad's side. I didn't even

156

know if I had aunts, uncles, or cousins from my mom's side. She never spoke about them. It felt as though it was meant for real Hispanic families who had large tribes that celebrated life's moments together. Then, there was the Catholic aspect of it all. You would have to go to a Catholic church and enroll in classes to even be allowed to have this ritual performed; we were not Catholic. I also struggled with the fact that I didn't speak Spanish, and these classes were only offered in Spanish. The ceremony, which included reading from a Spanish Bible and responding to the priest, would all have to be in Spanish. Finally, I knew it would be very expensive, and Pa was struggling to make ends meet. The chemo was beginning to wear him down, and he was missing more and more time at work, which meant smaller and smaller paychecks.

Instead, we opted for a small, regular birthday party at our apartment. My cousins, along with my best friends from church, my childhood bestie Gina, her mom Marie, and her sister Esther all showed up. Tía Sonia made me a fancy, custom album to memorialize my fifteenth birthday. We filled it with Polaroid pictures taken that day.

After we brought out the cake, and sang me happy birthday, they told me to make a wish. I wished for my Dad to beat cancer.

After everyone left that night, Pa and I began to reminisce about the times he would take me to Chuck E. Cheese. I celebrated several birthdays there. I loved the ball pit and the fun mechanical rides they had. I thanked him for a very special birthday, and we called it a night. Pa and I lay in my bed together, a queen-sized waterbed. I lay in the middle, horizontally across the bed, on my left side. In front of me was Pa, lying on his left side, in the fetal position. I was the big spoon. I wrapped my free arm around him and held him tight. I breathed in his cologne, Old Spice, my favorite on him.

With a high glow in our room, I could see Pa clearly. The shared bedroom window was not dressed with curtains; it was only set with thin blinds, which did not keep the light out. The commercial businesses behind the apartment complex used highly fluorescent security lighting, making it as bright as though a full moon sat right outside our window.

I began drifting off to sleep when suddenly, Pa spoke. He began telling me how proud of me he was and his dreams for my future.

"You're going to grow up, get married, have babies... Promise me you'll stay in church," he said.

Hot tears rolled down my cheeks like acid, my throat tight and muscles stiff. I didn't want him to feel my heart breaking, so with all my might, I kept it hidden. I steeled my stomach for strength and control over my voice as I whispered, "I promise."

Luis Was Here

Three months later, I didn't understand what the hospital bed delivered to our apartment meant. I had assumed it was a Medicaid benefit for those with cancer. Maybe Pa's doctors wanted him to be able to recover or be sick at home, versus making constant trips to the hospital. The bed was moved into our shared bedroom, up against the window; Pa's twin-sized bed was moved out to make space for it.

Soon after, he began consuming only homemade jugo naturales such as juiced carrots and oranges. He began sleeping more, for longer lengths of time, and was in visible discomfort. Then, a nurse showed up. I figured this, too, was a Medicaid benefit. Yet, I still didn't interpret the signs.

The nurses spent most of the day with Pa and then began administering oxygen and pain medications. At night, a male night nurse cared for my dad and helped him bathe.

A social worker showed up one afternoon. She said her job was to help take care of me as his next of kin. When she began asking me to confirm where I would live next, I didn't understand.

"Next?" I asked.

"When your father passes," she responded.

"How much time does he have left?"

"Maybe two weeks," the social worker stated bluntly.

159

Her words punched me in the gut. It made the nerves in my belly feel as though there was a tsunami-like devastation inside of me. The air escaped my lungs. My heart stopped beating. Suddenly, I felt like I weighed a thousand pounds.

I only had my dad for two weeks? Two weeks. Fourteen sleeps. After all the chemo, the special bed and nurses, after everything? Why couldn't he just get better? Why did cancer have to mean death? Did the surgery and chemo do nothing? I don't remember any of the conversations with the social worker after that.

Then one day, miraculously, Pa rose from his bed with some strength, and waltzed into the kitchen demanding food.

"This is it!" I thought excitedly. It felt as though he was experiencing a dramatic recovery after some rest, and now we could move on with our lives. The social worker was wrong.

It was the middle of the night when the nurse came to wake Erica and me. We slept on the living room floor to give Pa and the nurse the bedroom.

In a somber but kind voice, the nurse said, "It's time."

Erica quickly got up and proceeded to follow the nurse back into the bedroom. Not understanding the urgency and being a heavy sleeper, I closed my eyes and fell back asleep. Unsure of how much time had passed, I suddenly reawakened and realized where Erica had gone. I followed.

When I walked into the bedroom, Erica was holding Pa's hand, sorrow written on her face, tears streaming down. His body had expired.

I looked over at the clock; it was past 3 am.

He hadn't experienced a miracle; that final burst of energy was his end-of-life rally.

Early that morning, a morgue crew arrived to take my father's corpse. As the medics placed his body inside the black body bag, my aunts and cousins discussed whether his body should be taken out head or feet first because of superstitions.

Mom showed up. Erica and I were upset she hadn't visited before. During his final days, Pa called out for my mom. Because of this, we called her and urged her to come visit so he could say his peace. She told us her boyfriend didn't want her to go. Again, she chose the current man in her life over her family, even in a moment when her children needed her the most.

I packed and donated his clothes to the men's home, but I kept his suit. He was so proud to purchase the one to wear to church as an usher. It was his only suit. I wondered if, at the time of purchase, he thought about how it might serve a dual purpose.

I gathered one pair of underwear, an undershirt, one pair of socks, and his black penny loafer dress shoes to take to the funeral home.

"Oh, good, you included underclothing. Most people tend to forget to include that," the funeral director said jokingly.

I realized I packed the wrong type of socks. I gave the funeral director white crew socks for tennis shoes, not dress socks for penny loafers. A rush of guilt washed over me. Pa would have wanted me to pack the right socks, I cursed myself.

We discussed logistics and the amount owed, nearly fifteen thousand dollars. I had chosen the cheapest casket, but I wish there had been an even cheaper option. I had no idea how we were going to pay for it all.

While packing up the apartment, I discovered Pa wrote on the wall beside his bed, "Luis was here." I'm sure it was simply painted over in preparation for the next rent-paying tenant. But not erased, so likely still exists.

I thought Pa paid off the sofa and dining sets he brought home after Mom moved out. I would spray those couches with Febreeze a million times because it made our new-to-us hand-me-down couches smell fresh and clean. But after he passed and I had to move out, the furniture went back to its original owner, and I abandoned my waterbed.

Pa's body was on display in the funeral home for several days. Pa's father didn't get to make it in time to say goodbye. Getting a visa approved to travel from El Salvador to the United States was too long a process. So we held off burying his body until his dad arrived.

My aunts asked me if I wanted to continue living in the apartment with my grandpa. I was taken aback. I didn't know the man, I didn't speak Spanish, I didn't know how we would pay for rent, etc. It made no sense at all. I had to decline, not caring if they would be upset with me.

The photo we provided for the mortuary cosmetologist showed him at a healthy weight with full cheeks. To reenact this look, they filled my father's cheeks with some material to remove the gaunt, sunken appearance left from his dramatic weight loss. A wax-like substance was used on his lips to mimic a smile. Makeup was caked on to bring the color back to his skin. I was disappointed with how it turned out. That wasn't my dad. I did not want to visit the corpse. His soul was gone and all that was left was a rotting shell.

Mom and Erica took me shopping since I needed a funeral dress. We stopped in at Macy's at Sharpstown Mall, and after trying on a few options, I found a sleeveless, baggy black dress on the sales rack. It fit, it was cheap, so we bought it. Later that night, we dyed my hair from dark brown to a pretty auburn. I was pleased with how it complemented my skin tone. But when I saw my Tía Estella at the funeral home the next day, she didn't have a nice thing to say.

"You should be here with your father instead of dying your hair," she rebuked.

People grieve in different ways; not everyone will understand another's process, but that comment hurt. It did not make me a bad daughter. I did not believe that the shell of a body left in that casket was my father; it was only the suit his soul wore for a short time. My father was gone.

On the day of the funeral, I distinctly remember the smell of fresh flowers. I caught the scent before I saw the many arrangements sent by family and friends. I realized that I had never really smelled fresh flowers before that. The closest I came to fresh flowers was carnations given at school events. Even the bouquet Nancy gifted me didn't carry a strong scent. It must've been all of the Stargazer Lilies found in many of the arrangements. That day, I began to hate the scent of flowers.

Before the wake service could begin, the funeral director found me and mentioned the balance. Pastor Joe overheard and came over to hand me some cash that the church had raised; this still left a remaining balance of nearly fourteen thousand dollars. Then, Johnny Bang walked in. He fulfilled my dad's final wish and paid off the funeral costs.

I recognized many people from Pa's past. Old friends from past churches we attended, people from the neighborhood, and others. Pastor Joe's wife, Sister Gloria, created and passed out funeral programs, Pastor Joe performed the eulogy with an interpreter, and one of the gifted singers from our church sang a few of Pa's favorite praise and worship songs.

Before it came time for me to speak, I glanced around the room and spotted a beetle on the wall near the ceiling. I wondered if it was a Deathwatch Beetle, or even if Pa had reincarnated into the beetle and was observing his own funeral service. I also prayed over and over again for Pa to miraculously rise from the casket, like Lazarus from the Bible. I reminded myself I just needed faith the size of a mustard seed, like I was taught. I believed, prayed, and waited, but of course, he did not rise. The body was embalmed, so how could there be a miracle?

Then my name was announced. I had nothing prepared, so I had to wing it. Through tears, I reminded everyone that Pa would want me and each of them to continue living... or something like that. Honestly, it was a blur.

After the service, a few uncles and church members carried the casket into the hearse. The rest of us lined our cars behind it. Erica's car was directly behind the hearse with her as the driver, along with Mom and me as passengers.

The funeral procession was a sight. I appreciated the motorists stopping to make way for the procession led by officers on motorbikes. The caravan made its way from Bellaire funeral home, twenty-two miles up north to Earthman Cemetery.

When we parked, Erica said to me, "You should have driven." I had just obtained my driver's license. An achievement Pa set me up for.

164

We walked toward the tent for the final funeral service. I noticed the setup looked mediocre and second-rate. There were old, dirty, rusty bars used for the casket lowering mechanism, shoddy pieces of turf grass strewed about attempting to cover the fresh earth from recent digging, and unappealing and shabby mismatched metal folding chairs. I was extremely disappointed. I had envisioned a setup similar to what I had seen in movies; shiny polished steel with designed end accents connecting the bars, clean and fluffy turf grass laid in an organized and thoughtful manner, and well-maintained matching chairs or set with neatly cleaned pressed chair covers. I wondered if the fancy set up was an upgrade and due to our circumstances, we were forced to choose the cheap service.

After the final words from Pastor Joe, a plain brass cross was removed from the casket and handed to me. I was then instructed to toss my flowers onto the casket, and others followed suit. Then, the cemetery director thanked us all for coming, which was our cue to leave. Slightly taken aback by the abrupt ending, I asked Erica, "Aren't they supposed to lower the casket in front of us? Don't we toss the first dirt on top?"

"I don't know, baby," she responded, shrugging her shoulders.

The cemetery workers began dismantling the tent and folding up chairs, so we were all forced to stand aside. It was so unceremonious, and still, no one wanted to leave.

II

Part Two

After Death

Moving On

My father lost his battle with colon cancer the first week of June, the summer going into my sophomore year of high school. During the wake service, Mom and Erica approached me to ask if I was going to move back in with Mom. I had shared with Erica the night before that I would be moving in with my pastor; she didn't like that idea.

"No. I'm moving in with Pastor Joe. I promised Pa I would stay in church," I told them.

"Well, you can't do that. Mom, tell her she has to go back with you," Erica demanded.

"If she doesn't want to move in with me, she doesn't have to," Mom countered.

There it was again. The feeling of rejection, by my own mother. At my father's funeral. It stung that she didn't argue, just relented. She had never even met Pastor Joe, and she was allowing me to go live with strangers. I knew it had to have had something to do with her new beau. The one who supposedly didn't let her visit her dying daughters' father. We had already been living apart for three years. She was probably happy to be rid of me and not looking forward to raising a teenager. I really didn't want to live with her after that.

Only Erica seemed to care. But with everything going on, she respected my decision. She probably felt like this was a way for me to honor our dad and for me to heal.

A week and a half later, it was Father's Day. As soon as I got to church, I ignored everyone and quickly made my way inside. I knelt down in front of my seat and hid my face so others wouldn't see me cry. This is how we prayed before service began, so I hoped no one would take notice. Suddenly, I felt arms wrap around me. It was Angie. She sat there in silence, comforting me through my sorrow.

Pastor Joe lived in North Houston, which was zoned to Jersey Village High School in the Cypress-Fairbanks Independent School District. Because I transferred outside of Houston ISD, that meant that I was no longer eligible for my scholarship program.

When I spoke to the program mentors for guidance on ways to keep my scholarship, they blithely explained that I could do nothing except stay enrolled at Lee High School.

I hadn't realized it was mandatory to continue participating in their mentorship sessions and retreats. I didn't understand that I was accountable to this agreement to obtain the money I assumed I had already earned by winning the essay contest.

My world continued to crumble around me.

While it was a very kind gesture for Pastor Joe to take me in, it wasn't all I had hoped it would be. For starters, I was living in the back house with one other young woman. The old "men's home" that housed those who were seeking rehabilitation. The home was shabby and cold. It looked like it was built with men in mind. It wasn't a comfortable way of living. I would often sleep over in the main house, bunking with his daughters. Vero and Angie would even fight over whose bed I would sleep in. It was great for a few weeks, but I was still mourning the death of my father, and this didn't feel like home.

Lena

While Pa was still alive, there was another member of our church who was battling cancer. Lena had breast cancer, and so she and my dad built a sort of kinship. They could have the types of conversations that no one else could relate to. I imagine their conversations discussed pain, discomfort, worry, fear, hope, and faith.

Sometimes, Lena would attend church service in a wheelchair, being pushed faithfully by her then-husband, Luis (pronounced Louie). Sometimes, they would leave service early if she were experiencing sickness or discomfort.

Lena's son, Michael, was my youth pastor. Their family all lived in Alvin, Texas. Alvin was a long drive away from the North Houston church location, but they made the trek religiously a few days every week. One of Lena's daughters, Karen, would occasionally come to Sunday services.

It wasn't until my dad passed away that she approached me to say that I could reach out to her if I ever needed anything. From there, every week, she would ask me how I was doing and if I needed anything.

"Actually," I said, "I found a few hundred dollars hidden in one of my dad's blazers. I don't have a bank account, so could you hold it for me?"

Lena became my unofficial bank. If I needed twenty dollars to have lunch after church, she would give it to me. Before my dad's government-issued LoneStar benefits card was canceled, I learned from my sister that there was a cash allowance, so I withdrew seventy dollars to add to my "savings."

When I saw Lena again, I eagerly handed her the cash; she was excited that I was finally giving her a "deposit."

Once, I confided in her that I wasn't truly happy living at the Pastor's home. And by home, I'm referring to the second house on his property that used to be the rehab house for men. The construction wasn't very clean or professional-looking. I imagined that those in the program had built it.

This dwelling had an odd bathroom featuring urinals and short doors for the stalls, a kitchen that felt like it was designed for a jail room, and no private bedrooms. Melissa, a young woman from Colorado, slept in the same communal space as I did. There was no privacy, even for mourning.

About a week later, I saw Lena at church, and she waved excitedly at me. With a big smile, she hobbled over and said, "I spoke with Luis, and he agreed that it would be fun if you moved in with us!"

I was not expecting an invitation to move in with her and was at a loss for words. She probably saw the confusion on my face and said, "Well, aren't you excited? We are!"

I saw Lena the following week, and we spoke in the children's church; it was my Sunday to cover the kiddos while their parents attended the big church for service.

I gave her my answer, and she ran to tell her husband. They both returned, and she walked in, beaming with excitement to say, "Say hello to your new Pa!" But she pronounced it, "Paw," in her South Texas accent.

Ouch. My heart hurt at hearing those words. I had only lost my dad weeks prior, and her words felt as though they insinuated that I could simply replace my father and betray him. I understand that wasn't her intention. Lena was so happy to open up her home and heart to me.

Not wanting to be rude, I quickly masked my emotions, slapped on a smile, looked up, and said, "Hi, Dad." I could never call anyone by the same name I called my real father. I hated myself for even calling him "dad."

Soon after, I moved my belongings from the "home" into Luis and Lena's apartment in South Houston. Their apartment seemed fancy. Lena lined the standard built-in bookshelves with black felt to display her menagerie of crystal figurines. Luis lined the baseboards with a wide, dark grey, vinyl-like material that grounded the place. These subtle changes made such an impact that when the leasing office wanted to tour potential renters, they used Lena's apartment as an example. I thought it was more of a "luxury" community, but I was wrong. In the short span that I lived there, the FBI raided neighboring units twice due to drug and or criminal activity. The apartment wasn't roach-infested, so to me, that was luxury.

Because I no longer lived on Pastor Joe's property, I needed a plan to move my dad's truck, which had been parked in the pastor's home driveway. Lena's then-son-in-law had been searching for a low-cost vehicle, so she negotiated the sale on my behalf. He paid in installments. With this sale, I thought I would still see Pa's truck from time to time, but not too long after, Karen, Lena's daughter, divorced her then-husband. I never saw Pa's truck again.

The transition had been smooth for the most part. Lena registered me for school in her district, took me shopping for back-to-school clothes and supplies using the money from the truck sale, and got my haircut. The enrollment process into Pasadena's school district was interesting. During the interview, the Superintendent asked me,

"If you lived on your own as a fifteen-year-old, would you be able to do that?"

"No," I responded.

"And why not? Why wouldn't you be able to live on your own?"

"Because I'm a minor and I don't have a job."

"Exactly! She is the first student to answer that correctly."

Seemed like a dumb question and a lazy answer to me. Not sure why that was the determining factor but, it got me into South Houston High School.

Lena introduced me to the rest of her family. I even agreed to watch her other daughter, Angela's, triplet girls at her Alvin home for the rest of that summer. It would be cheaper for Angela and her husband to hire me than a standard live-in Nanny. And it was a good way for me to earn spending money.

One day, as the three of us were adjusting to this new life, Lena was in my room chatting with me when Luis walked in. He seemed sheepish, and his face was a little red. Lena encouraged him to say what he needed to.

"I was cleaning the restroom the other day, and I just wanted to say that I think it's better to flush the toilet paper when you've done a number two," Luis said with his hands held out in front of his chest, gesturing and moving rapidly from nerves, eyes darting everywhere and avoiding contact with mine.

"In some countries, they don't flush the paper because of bad plumbing, but you don't have to worry about that here," Lena added in a tone that meant to come off as educational and sympathetic.

I sat there a little dumbfounded. Had I not been flushing my toilet paper? Did he maybe see dark period-stained pads wrapped in toilet paper and confuse the two? What was the country comment about? Did she think my family came from uncivilized societies since they weren't natural-born citizens of the U.S. and, therefore, thought less of them? Of me?

Again, being young and not wanting to be rude as a guest in their home, I responded, "Okay, I'll be sure to flush the paper from now on." I didn't ask questions or argue; I just obliged.

I realized Karen actually visited Lena a lot more than I had assumed. Since I rarely saw her at Sunday services, I foolishly assumed those were the only times Karen and Lena would meet. Karen really welcomed me with open arms. She was both charming and a firecracker. I really enjoyed her company and looked up to her. She didn't shy away from standing up for herself or others. She didn't filter her emotions, staying true to herself and sharing her exact thoughts. Karen was also a great cook, and you could taste the love in her food, especially in her handmade, fresh flour tortillas. I enjoyed spending time with her and her new beau, Christopher. I would stay over at their place and annoy them with my silly choreographed dances around the house. Chris and Karen would help take me to my cheer events and even watch me perform. They felt like family.

One evening, Michael, Lena's son and my youth pastor, offered me a ride home because Lena skipped Sunday service since she wasn't feeling well. Michael began making small talk and eventually asked how I liked living with his mom.

"Just be careful with how much you believe. I hate to tell you this, but we don't really believe my mom had cancer," Michael said.

Michael proceeded to explain that Lena never allowed anyone to join her for any medical appointments, that the letters from the doctor were never on official letterhead, and several other alarming examples. I sat stunned and speechless, but ultimately decided never to bring it up. I was enjoying my new school, friends, and social activities. I also didn't want to bring up any discussion regarding cancer.

On a separate occasion, when I was riding with Luis, he explained to me that Lena had previously exhibited symptoms of multiple personality disorder. Lena would sleepwalk during the night, and her feet and bed sheets would be covered in dirt, leaves, and twigs in the morning. He made it sound as though it had happened many years prior, and so I convinced myself that she was better now and no longer dealing with this issue.

During one of Lena's fainting spells, Karen sat by her side for support. Lena had coincidentally fainted onto the sofa and was lying back. Eyes closed, she began to mutter. Lena began speaking to someone on the "other side." Some words we could understand; others sounded as though she were speaking in tongues. Her hands would move and gesture as though someone were directly in front of her or she were reaching for what her mind's eye could see. I sat in silence, confused and unsure of how to help.

As Karen grew tired of the antics, she would say things to purposefully make Lena laugh, thus ending Lena's momentary "medical issue" and forcing Lena to wake up or return to reality. This also proved that Lena wasn't in a trance, speaking with spirit guides or heavenly beings, but that she was faking. I wondered if she faked each time.

In the early 90s, when Lena's son was falling into the wrong crowd, she opened her home to troubled youth. Michael and his friends would stay at her home, attend church, do chores, and stay sober. As her outreach grew, the infamous Mattress Mack, aka Jim McIngvale, a Houston philanthropist and owner of Gallery Furniture, donated and delivered multiple bunk beds to help ensure the boys in Lena's care had comfort and space. Some of those boys kept in touch with Lena.

The Lena I was living with wanted the best for me, too. She helped me tap into my feminine side as a young teen. She noticed when I moved in and began to unpack that I only had men's socks to wear because my dad and I shared socks. I hadn't realized there were socks made specifically for girls and women. She helped me buy new clothes because she loved to shop. People took notice of my little transformation, and it lifted my confidence.

During tax season, Lena returned to work at an office in Alvin, where she made great money. Her customers would tip her lots of money, even hundreds, and all in cash! She would then take me shopping at Melrose, K-mart, and other stores, but taught me how to look for flattering cuts. I thought Melrose was a fancy boutique.

She supported all my extracurricular activities in school. She drove me to all my UIL theater competitions, encouraged me during my drill team and cheer tryouts, and cheered me on during all of my performances.

Lena gave me permission to drive her car, and so I gained more experience by driving around our neighborhood in her small sedan. While driving around, out of the blue, Lena said to me, "You are so smart and you are a good person, I know you're going to be successful.

I can see you wearing a white lab coat someday."

I was flourishing at school, making new friends, and growing in the ministry. Overall, I felt like life was good and stress-free. I could finally just be a normal teenager.

Then, Lena dropped the news. She was filing for divorce from Luis.

I really liked Luis. He was respectful, kind, and funny. He took me to Memorial Park, where we walked through the horse and mountain bike trails. It felt like we were transported to an actual forest and not in Houston anymore. I really enjoyed our time together.

Afterward, Lena shared with me that Luis was secretly a homosexual and would hook up with strange men in that same forested area we had hiked. Supposedly, he had been busted by the police once, too. Solicitation was the alleged crime.

A part of me didn't believe her because it felt as though she wanted to purposely paint him in a bad light and also win me over. It was just strange. Why share that information with a young girl?

Luis moved out, and it was pretty uneventful. I don't even remember saying goodbye.

Although I hadn't known her long and lived with her for even less, Lena had only seemed sane to me. It was hard to believe that she could orchestrate such detailed lies and behavior. To fake cancer is immoral.

After Luis moved out, Lena began behaving as though she were sick again. Because she didn't have the energy, I was forced to ask friends, teammates, and neighbors for rides to school events. Eventually, she stopped taking us to church. The energy shifted.

Perhaps to cheer herself up, Lena then began going out on her own on weekends, and she quickly met a new man. She was really excited about dating him and once drove me over to meet him. He didn't own a car, so we had to pick him up. I'm not really sure what to call the compound he lived in because it wasn't a typical apartment complex. It wasn't even a storage unit; it was some structure made of cinder blocks, corrugated metal, tarps, and other random materials. There were multiple units like this, and they shared concrete walls. I thought it was some sort of shop where cars or other goods were repaired, but people were actually living there. It looked like the type of housing you would see in an undeveloped country.

I moved from the front passenger seat to the back seat. When he got into the car, he kissed Lena on the lips. She was beaming, and he turned around to introduce himself to me. He only spoke Spanish. I didn't speak Spanish, so I only responded with "Hola."

Things moved really quickly between Lena and her new beau. Soon, he was spending nights over at our apartment. She was now taking him shopping, out to dinners, etc. Then, he officially moved in.

I quickly became uncomfortable with how things had progressed. I had promised my dad that I would continue going to our church after he passed, which is why I had moved in with my pastor and then Lena instead of my mom, but we weren't attending services anymore. Lena was no longer as supportive of my extracurricular activities, leaving me alone at events and having to bum rides. It became apparent to me that her new beau had all her attention, and it felt all too reminiscent of how my mom put the men in her life before me. I wasn't happy anymore.

I decided to call my sister and ask her to help me move back home. Without question, she showed up that weekend with a U-Haul. When Erica arrived, I went into Lena's room to let her know. I can't recall the exact words she said to me; perhaps I purposely blocked it from my memory, but I know it hurt. My eyes, nose, and throat stung as I forced myself not to cry. Lena stayed in her room the entire time Erica and I were loading up the truck. When we were done, I didn't go back to say goodbye. We drove away.

Alief

After leaving Lena's apartment, Erica brought me to Mom's two-bedroom condo. This wasn't the Gulfton Ghetto, but this neighborhood actually looked worse. There were several prostitutes roaming Club Creek in broad daylight, mid-afternoon, the roads were poorly maintained, and all of the apartment buildings appeared dilapidated.

Erica and I quickly unloaded the U-Haul pickup truck, and then it was time for Erica to take the rental back and return home to her family. We said our goodbyes.

I sat in my mom's apartment alone, waiting for her to arrive. Since it had been a few years since we lived together, I expected a warm homecoming embrace and welcome. But when the front door unlocked, her boyfriend walked in first. I didn't even know she had a boyfriend. He very awkwardly said, "Hola," and quickly made his way to her bedroom.

Then she walked in, said a few words, and followed him. I was left sitting alone in the living room, feeling utterly emotionally confused.

"I guess she isn't happy to have me move back," I figured.

Deep exhale. Her priorities hadn't changed.

Mom later emerged from her bedroom and brought me sheets to cover the sofa for me to sleep on. I thanked her, and she went back into her room. Not wanting to sleep in the living room covered in cat fur and

181

having a strong smell of cat urine, I got up, went into my room, and started setting up my bed. No one offered to help.

After we registered me at Alief Hastings High School, I received the bus route information and prepped my alarm so that I would be at the bus stop at 6 am. To my surprise, Mom woke up and walked me to the bus stop that first day. She even waited with me until the bus came. She did this for a few days until I excused her because I felt comfortable enough to go on my own.

I would pack my lunch and sit alone in the cafeteria. Packing a lunch in a cute bag was cool at South Houston, but at Hastings, it seemed nerdy. So I began to ditch the cafeteria and would make my way to the library. My safe haven. I could hide my loneliness behind a book and eat in peace.

There were already a few *Harry Potter* books out by this time, and the waiting list to check out any of them was weeks or even months long. I even applied for a public library card in hopes of getting a better chance at securing a copy. In my early years of high school, I read more Christian-focused literature in hopes it would help me on my spiritual journey, but after Pa passed and I was no longer active in the church, I turned back to secular young-adult reads. I was occupying myself with the *Sweep* Series by Cate Tiernan about a young girl who discovers she's a natural witch. I just needed something to fill a void, and it was entertaining. Plus, reading about forbidden witchcraft at this point in life was enticing.

I learned that my old cheer squad would be competing at Reliant Stadium, and I desperately wanted to go. I missed my team. My sister drove me to the event, paid for our tickets, and watched hours of cheer competitions, just so I could watch their two and a half minute routine.

I knew the whole routine to SoHo's choreography, but noticed they reconfigured some of the formations because of the change in the number of cheerleaders. Even so, my old team killed it, and I was so proud of them.

Erica was supportive and stayed until the very end so that I could reunite with my squad and catch up with everyone. On the way home, I was going on and on about how they performed so well, but Erica felt Sharpstown High School's cheer team had the best performance. I agreed. Sharpstown didn't place in the competition that day, and we speculated whether the Sharpstown squad being majority Black students with more of an urban routine, had affected their chances.

A high school girl in the same apartment complex recognized me from the school bus and invited me to hang out. I took her offer, and I would visit her apartment from time to time. She was sweet, and while she wasn't the type of friend I sought out, I appreciated her kindness. She would talk to me about boys and makeup, offer fashion advice, and braid my hair. I didn't particularly want to dress the same way she did, but I was quickly learning that the preppy style I was accustomed to from my previous school did not match the trend at my new school.

Once I started to dress like the others, even borrowing my sister's way-too-small but cute pair of black Nike sneakers to try and fit in, I began to get noticed. Kids in classes who previously ignored me began to ask me about my previous school and my background. Girls would invite me to have lunch with them. Boys would ask for my phone number. This was all new to me. Suddenly, I felt like the "it girl" because I was new and "mysterious."

It was at this time that I began to rebel, and I asked my mom to take me to get a tattoo.

Mom found out her boyfriend had been cheating on her, so they broke up. She began a friendship with one of the neighbors. This guy would take us out to eat, out shopping, and help Mom fix things around the apartment. She had no real interest in dating him and was treating him the same way she treated her old customers.

Mom had mentioned that I was wanting a tattoo, and the neighbor suggested an artist. Being sixteen, I needed a parent's permission, so I couldn't go solo. Mom convinced him to take us to the studio where his friend worked. I was naive as hell and had no idea what I was doing. I told the artist I like dolphins, so he showed me a page in a book of different dolphin images. I chose one, and he stenciled it. When he returned to show me, I assumed it was a rough sketch and that the finished work would be as good as the image I chose. I was wrong. It was a terrible tattoo, and I had it placed on my lower back, aka the tramp stamp. I didn't care at the time that it was imperfect; I was happy to finally have a tattoo. I then went on to get my tongue pierced.

Everyone at school took notice and would ask me where I got my work done. I would give vague answers and never mention that my mommy took me.

I picked up a part-time job after school where I earned $6.10 an hour. My checks were typically two hundred or so dollars every two weeks. To me at the time, that was a lot of money, but it didn't go very far. I paid a percentage at Fiesta Mart to cash my paycheck because I did not have a bank account, and then I would use the cash to pay the phone, light, water, and any other bills my mom had. Whatever remained was used to fill up the Camaro with gas and grab a bite to eat.

It felt good being able to get my mom's accounts up-to-date versus having a rolling past due amount and constant mail of warning letters regarding having services cut off. I hated coming home from school only to find we were without electricity when I had homework to do.

Study in the dark, shower in the dark, and so on. We only had so many candles.

It also gave me a sense of responsibility and control. I began to really understand that if I worked hard, I could build a better life.

Mom later took a job at Taco Cabana. She would work the late-night shift and wake me when she brought home leftovers, mostly consisting of roasted chicken and flour tortillas. One afternoon, I stopped by the restaurant to visit her, and when I walked in, I saw she was being trained on the register. I stood back and watched as Mom struggled to get accustomed to it, but her trainer was very patient. Mom was timid, shy, and lacked confidence. Witnessing this small moment helped me understand why she never took a "normal" job.

It even brought me back to when I was in the third or fourth grade, when Erica was studying to obtain her GED at the local Bayland Park Community Center. Mom also decided to try her hand at obtaining a GED. She would pick me up from school, and we would drive to this community center where she would attempt to work through her assignments. These assignments consisted of reading, writing, and math problems. I would help my mom by doing the assignments for her. Luckily for me, the math problems featured adding, subtracting, multiplying, dividing and fractions, which were levels I was familiar with. Unfortunately for my mom, I was unable to help her with her final exams, and she therefore did not pass.

How good a job or income could my mother even obtain without a proper education? This realization helped give me a small glimpse into understanding why we lived in poverty.

Coming to the end of my Senior year, the pain of my father's passing still raw, along with all the life changes, put me in a mood where I didn't care to attend graduation. I just wanted school to be over with.

My melancholy was not to be confused with "senioritis." I just realized that everything I had worked towards in my high school career was all for nothing. I lost my college scholarship, because I moved again mid-semester, I couldn't try out for any cheer or dance squad, and because I transferred districts, many of my credits wouldn't apply, and I had to take even more classes to make up for it. What was even the point anymore? I had zero motivation left.

As I counted the weeks until school was out, we received pamphlets from Balfour, the local commencement services company that sells everything grad-related: caps and gowns, class rings, senior photos, the list goes on. When I perused the offerings, I was astounded by the prices. Who could afford to spend hundreds on a class ring?! It's not like it was a wedding ring. I wasn't even attached to this particular high school. And the cost of the cap and gown, which are made of plastic-like materials, was also too damn high. Couldn't students just rent a set? You only wear it for a few hours and never wear it again. It was all so ridiculous.

I made the mistake of showing Erica the pamphlet, and her reaction was the opposite of mine. She was excited to see the options for things to buy for seniors. She wanted to order me one of everything! I had to convince her to restrain herself.

"It's all plastic junk! The same things you can get from the 99 cent store!" I insisted.

Since Erica opted for her GED, she didn't have an opportunity to participate in a graduation ceremony, and I felt she was living vicariously through me. She paid for my polyester cap and gown, that felt as cheap as a Halloween Costume, my Y2K mall glamour photo shoot, and more. Although I was never confident enough to depend on my parents to be there for me, Erica always showed up.

Road to Success

I had dreams growing up; dreams of being a professional cheerleader or becoming a backup dancer for Britney Spears and Janet Jackson. I also loved science and dreamed of working in a lab.

I started working at the age of sixteen while in high school. My career journey began in entry-level roles, such as cashier in stores including Party City and Pep Boys. After high school, I became a bilingual customer service representative at a call center for TXU Energy. Here, I would work from 6 am to midnight to rack up as much overtime as possible. And as a freshman in college, I became a receptionist.

For the receptionist role, I was hired by a local family-owned jewelry store through a staffing agency. During the interview, the hiring manager asked, "What's your credit score?" This question was a part of the interview process because someone with bad credit may not be trusted near high-value items. I proudly responded, "Pretty good. I just bought myself a new car for the first time and was told my score was 614. My boyfriend said it was higher than his mom's."

Growing up, I always heard the term "credit." It would be a focus topic during commercials, in conversations my family had, promoted in stores, and so on. Credit is how people are able to buy things now and pay later. It's different than layaway because on credit, you're able to take the items with you and pay later, versus leaving the items to slowly pay off the balance in order to finally obtain the products.

Credit scores are gauged on how well you can be trusted to pay loans back based on your payment history. Good credit means you can be trusted with more money loaned, whereas having bad credit means you aren't approved for as much. Then there are interest rates which is how the company loaning the money makes a profit. These rates can be very high for those with little or bad credit history.

I first opened a Foley's department store credit card while working there as a cashier. I was earning roughly six dollars an hour, so my paychecks were only two to three hundred dollars after taxes. Therefore, I would only charge approximately fifty dollars at a time; that was the limit I set for myself, even though I was approved for more. I chose this method to ensure I could pay off the balance each month. I wanted to avoid a rolling balance and a high interest rate. I made sure to educate myself regarding the billing cycle in order to pay off my balance ahead of the due dates and avoid any interest.

I was careful with my money. If a family member ever asked me to help co-sign for a loan, my answer was and is always, "No." This may seem heartless, cruel, or selfish, but when an adult older than you needs a co-signer, that's typically not a good sign. And when you know this person has bad financial habits, then that's the only sign you should pay attention to. It's incredibly difficult to do, and guilt will set in, but you must stand your ground. It's your future at stake; they already had their chance.

I always say, "I don't come from money, all I have is my name," meaning my family was not wealthy. I didn't have a financial safety net or anything of value. All I had was my credit score to begin with and I wasn't about to ruin my chance of leaving the ghetto.

When I started college, I opened my first official credit card with Discover. Although I had applied for FAFSA (Free Application for Federal Student Aid), I was only granted very little. At the time of my application for student aid, my mother wasn't working, but I was employed, so I applied as Head of Household. My meager income had to cover the cost of utilities, food, and gas, which left me with nothing extra for school. The student aid amount I was granted didn't even cover the cost of my classes, let alone the necessary supplies.

That's where my Discover card came in. I paid HCC (Houston Community College) for the remaining balance of my classes with my credit card and then took my syllabi from said classes to shop at the student college store. It was there that I purchased the required supplies such as textbooks, scantrons, blue books, calculators, and more. After charging a few hundred dollars to my new Discover card, I felt extremely anxious. I knew I would not have the money to pay it off before the next billing cycle and that I would be hit with interest fees on top of it.

Each month, my goal was to pay off at least one hundred dollars, but the interest rate was so high, that it seemed as though I barely made a dent in the accrued balance. After months of payments and getting the balance down to a decent amount, a new semester would begin, and I had to charge all new purchases on my Discover card all over again. Some classes had the option of buying pre-owned or old edition textbooks which cost less, but other classes, such as the math and science courses, required new books that were accompanied by web codes to access online learning platforms. It's a vicious cycle, but I refused to apply for student loans and bury myself in even more debt. It just meant that I couldn't afford to take as many classes in a single semester, prolonging my graduation.

After visiting with the school counselor to try to figure out the best path for me, I set a goal to study nursing. The plan was first to become a registered nurse, work to earn enough to return to school, and study genetics, specializing in the study and research of oncogenes to help find a cure for cancer. After Pa's death, I wanted to help find a cure so that others did not have to suffer the same way we did. Unfortunately, the pharmacology course final exam took me out of the running to become a registered nurse. I guess taking the short summer course was a bad idea.

I then shifted my degree plan and focused on general studies. I only attended school part-time while having to work full-time and, at times, even held additional part-time jobs.

It took seven long years to finally earn my associates degree. By then, I didn't even care to walk at graduation and skipped the ceremony. I left my degree certificate in the cardboard mailer it arrived in, not caring to open and display it.

While I was disappointed in my education journey, at the same time, I was gaining traction in my career. I was still working for the family-owned jewelry store and had been promoted from receptionist to personal assistant to sales assistant to marketing assistant and finally, marketing manager.

During the 2020 COVID pandemic, my husband and I relocated to Austin, Texas, and I joined the Whole Foods Market corporate team. From there, I followed one of the Whole Foods' executive leaders to another local Austin company, only to be poached by the previous Whole Foods' Vice President to her new company, where she offered me the role of Chief of Staff. Later, I learned that the jewelry store I worked for in Houston for fifteen years was set to open a new store in Austin; the family asked me back and offered me the role of Director of

Operations. It was a complete full-circle moment in my career, from a college student receptionist to opening and operating a new branch of business for one of the largest independent jewelry retailers in the U.S., Zadok Jewelers.

Ascending from entry-level earnings of six dollars an hour to the upper-management level earning six figures took lots of hard work, determination, sacrifice, and grit. I knew from a very young age that I did not want to remain living in the ghetto for the rest of my life. I knew education was my key to success. Although I didn't become a pro backup dancer or earn the cool science degrees to work in a lab like I envisioned, I attribute my success to my studies, my love of reading, and hard work.

My goal now is to earn and save enough for early retirement, so that I can open a small business to support with passive income. This will afford me the opportunity to spend more time at home and traveling with my husband, Jose during our golden years.

Together, Jose and I aligned on our life goals and understood and respected each other's hard work and sacrifice. Now, we own multiple properties, can afford beautiful vacations, and are in a place to help our families when needed.

All this to say, I can confidently suggest that the keys to success are available for you to take. Here are my humble suggestions:

1. **Read Often**: Books will take you places you never imagined and teach you things you may never otherwise have an opportunity to learn.
2. **Be Mindful with Spending**: Teach yourself financial literacy and stick to your goals.

3. **Avoid Teen or Unwanted Pregnancy**: Family planning services are under attack during the current political administration, but at the time I am writing this, they are still available. Take advantage of these, sometimes free, resources if you need them.

4. **Find the Right Partner**: Choose someone who will support your goals, align with them, and work equally towards contributing to your success.

5. **Work Hard**: Have integrity, be honest, take accountability, and be prepared to make sacrifices. Just be sure it's for the right reasons.

6. **Be True to Yourself**: Maintain a healthy work/life balance. You work to live, not live to work. Things won't always go according to plan, but you must pick yourself up and keep pushing forward. Life comes at you when you least expect it, that's why having a safety cushion and backup plans are always necessary.

You can do it. I believe in you.

Breaking the Cycle

I learned the history of my parents later in life. I learned about my dad's early life, before me, through my Tía Sonia. I learned about my mom's childhood from a random phone call on a Sunday evening with her in my late thirties. These revelations brought me so much understanding. I was able to sympathize and comprehend that they, too, were victims of trauma. That any of their poor parenting traits were not a purposeful form of punishment or neglect, but an effect of their own deep-rooted trauma.

When you're a child, you look to your parents as though they're old and wise, having all the answers. But my parents were in their early twenties when they had me, and had no clue what they were doing. They did not have the familial or cultural support to raise a family. They did not have the financial security to even care for themselves. They did not have a solid foundation to build anything on. The odds were stacked against them from the beginning.

My parents did not have access to therapy, and as much as they tried to heal through their individual spiritual journeys, it was too late for Erica and me. I understand that now.

My dad showed his love by cooking, cleaning, teaching, providing emotionally and spiritually. He made delicious meals such as milanesa served with rice, beans, tortillas, avocado, and queso fresco, or caldo de pollo filled with veggies and seasoned to perfection. My favorite breakfast was a toasted bagel with cream cheese and avocado. My dad made avocado toast before it was popular.

Although financially poor by economic standards, I felt rich. I was rich in love. As a young child, even when my father was absent, I knew he loved me. When we were able to reunite, he would show me the inside of his wallet that always featured a picture of me. He would show it off to other people. I was his pride and joy. I'm grateful for the final years we shared.

My mother calls on occasion to apologize for things she remembers that oddly enough, I don't. But I appreciate the gesture all the same. During the process of journaling and turning those entries into this manuscript, I learned to forgive her.

Under a Cancer full moon, I wrote my mom a letter about all the things I was angry with her for. I burned it, and washed the ashes away with water. This was my ritual to let go of the resentment I harbored in my heart, and to accept her for the flawed human she is. We are all flawed in our own ways.

Jose understood and was supportive when I made the decision not to have children. I did not want to repeat any of the mistakes my parents made with me. I once told my sister, "Mom should have never had kids." I said that out of anger and resentment. I still believe in that statement, only now from a different perspective. I wish my mom hadn't had us in her teens and early twenties. I wish she had an opportunity to live a full, carefree life. I wish she had met good men, and not abusive drunkards, drug addicts and cheats. She deserved better.

I was lucky to have many pseudo-maternal figures in my life, including Erica, Doña Marie, Gina's mom, Marie, Becky's mom, Sylvia, Nancy, and Lena. All these women made an impact on my upbringing in various ways. I'm grateful to all of them.

Sadly, Doña Marie, Lena, and Pastor Joe have all passed. Doña Marie outlived my dad by decades, even though he would jokingly ask, "She's still alive?!" Lena's passing was unexpectedly predicted: "Someone like a mother figure will pass, but it's not your mom," the tarot reader told me. I was shocked when, days later, I opened social media and saw the post with a link to her obituary. Pastor Joe's death was particularly difficult. He taught me that we have three father figures in life: our earthly father, our spiritual father, and our heavenly father. He was a spiritual leader to both me and my dad. He's even buried in the same cemetery as Pa; I take comfort in that.

There were times in life when I could have given up hope and made decisions that would have led me down the wrong path. Statistics regarding young Latin students in the 90s held harsh predictions for our futures, but I refused to become a statistic. I knew there was so much more life could offer. All I needed to do was keep pushing, trying, and hoping.

Today, I no longer live in poverty. In fact, I feel pretty damn rich. I have a husband who loves me and shows his love in ways that help to fill the gaping hole in my heart after losing my dad. Together, we have built a beautiful life consisting of building our dream home, being able to treat ourselves to vacations a few times a year, and spoiling our pets. We have supportive, loving families and an amazing group of friends. We are both leaders in our companies, and we encourage each other to keep working hard and celebrate our accomplishments.

Here's to breaking generational trauma!

Acknowledgments

I would not have written this memoir without the encouragement, support, patience, and love of my dear husband, Jose.

Chalamalla, you not only planted the seed of writing in me, but you watered and nurtured it, too. Thank you for giving me all the tools I didn't even know I needed to accomplish this project. You are my soulmate, and I love you more than words could ever express.

To my sister, who is always there for me when I need her.

Sister, thank you for revisiting some of these childhood memories with me so that I had a clearer perspective to share with my readers. Thank you for always showing up for me, especially when it shouldn't have been your responsibility to do so. I am confident because I know you will always have my back, no matter what. I love you.

To my Tía Sonia, who helped me connect with my father's past.

Gracias por compartir conmigo detalles del pasado de mi padre. Me ayudo a comprenderlo y conocerlo mejor. TKM!

To all my friends who followed my writing journey, hyping me up and encouraging me along the way, thank you!

Angie, through this writing journey, you listened to me cry during my emotional releases and provided valuable advice when needed.

Diana, you gave thoughtful and positive feedback when I shared previews of my work, and gave me praise when I hit small milestones along the way.

Anita, your constant, uplifting admiration strengthened my determination to write this in hopes of becoming a role model for younger women. We're both Mexi-doran, and I genuinely love how you've always made me feel included and welcomed in your family.

Liz, thank you for helping connect me with my Mexican roots - from Spanish words and idioms, to lending your mom's help in teaching me how to make Mexican tamales, to inviting me to my first Posada. You gave me access to our culture, and I'm so grateful.

Thank you to my past leader, Jessica Keller, for suggesting that my book will be a *New York Times Best Seller!*

Jess, your belief in me taught me to begin seeing my own potential. Without your support in my career advancement, I may not have the career testimony I share today.

Thank you to the Zadok Family for trusting in me, and giving me the opportunity to grow with the business. It's been an honor.

To Jayla Balderas, I've said it before and I'll say it again, you are a God send!

Jay, thank you for reaching out and stepping in to guide me through the process of preparing and marketing my book. You held my hand, even through an extremely tight (nearly unrealistic) goal and deadline. You helped make the experience so much easier than it would have been otherwise. I'm in awe of the young woman you've grown into and am excited to see where your life takes you.

Special thanks to my editor, Lia Ottaviano, who helped me improve my writing and style.

Lia, you were the first to read my manuscripts (in all forms) and your feedback regarding my story was so uplifting and powerful, it brought me to tears and truly solidified my faith in that I was, and am, a writer.

Shout-out to my graphic designer, Lucero Leon. I wanted to support and work with another female Latin creator, and Jayla led me to Lucero.

Lucero, thank you for creating art beyond my imagination. I have found so much meaning in the cover and hope others see it, too.

Epilogue

An inspiration for writing this memoir was the search for a story like my own. I looked for books by other Latinas, hoping to see myself reflected in their words, but I couldn't find my experience on the page.

Many of their stories spoke of migrating to the U.S., learning English as a second language, and being raised by both hard-working parents who provided, disciplined, and expected much. I respected those stories, but I could not relate.

The book that resonated most with me was *The Glass Castle* by Jeannette Walls. Her memoir of dysfunctional parents, an unorthodox upbringing, and ultimate success mirrored parts of my own life. Yet even then, I didn't see the entirety of my experience reflected.

That's why I wrote this book. I want a reader to finish these pages and think, *"Wow, I'm not alone,"* or even, *"This feels like a story about my life."* No two lives are the same, but there are hundreds of thousands of first-generation Americans who didn't grow up with the so-called "typical" upbringing. And for young adolescents still in the thick of it, I want to offer hope: you can come out on top. You don't have to live the same life you were born into. You can write your own story.

My story takes place in Houston, Texas, where I was born and raised. A diverse city, a true melting pot, filled with immigrants from around the globe. I wrote this memoir with the first-gens in mind: those who grew up as I did, those who are still finding their way, and those who want a glimpse into this life of ours.

Growing up, I often wondered if anyone else at school had a parent addicted to drugs. If anyone else witnessed domestic violence, endured abuse, or felt like a burden. If you've ever felt any of this, then you and I are not alone.

Thank you for allowing me to share my story with you. May it bring comfort, understanding, and the reminder that healing and hope are always possible.